# ALPHA MALE STRATEGIES

*The Alpha Male to becoming a women magnet.*

*Charisma, Psychology of Attraction, Charm.*

*Richard  Gray*

Table of Contents

# CREATING YOUR OWN REALITY

Your world is what you perceive it to be. On the Internet, you can find an immense range of beliefs and ideas, and all of those beliefs are supported by people's own observations.

For example, many religious sites talk about God as if it is obvious that He exists, while atheists say that does not make sense. Read in-depth, and you will find interesting arguments for both views. How can that be that both sides are right? It is because each person has their own vision of reality.

What if a leg is broken? That's bad? You're probably thinking, "Of course it's bad, damn it." But suppose you were a British soldier in 1914 and that broken leg luckily prevented you from being cannon fodder on the Western Front. Then you would thank heaven for his broken leg and his crutches!

Here's the detail: reality is what you perceive it to be. There is no objective reality. Everything is open to interpretation. What would you think of a rainy day? You will have a completely different perspective depending on whether you want to go on a picnic or a farmer suffering through a drought.

Therefore, you have the power to see the world the way you want. You can have your own reality, your own framework of things.

A person with a weak reality is consumed by the perceptions of the world of others.

A person with a strong reality is unaffected by others' perceptions and instead drags them into his world.
Let's say you go to a nightclub and have trouble finding a place to park. A beta that allows external factors to control it will be disturbed by this. But you can come up with a way to keep yourself from being disturbed. Not finding a place to park means there will be many people in the clubs, which means many more women.

Have you ever got caught in traffic? That's not so bad, because it's an opportunity to take a break, relax, meditate, and maybe listen to some music. You don't have to join the rest of the pack by getting upset. You have the power to have a positive perception of events.

Now let's look at what kind of frame you have when talking about yourself. You want to have the framework in which you are an award that women want to win.

# THE ART OF FLIRTING BASED ON CONFIDENCE AND GOOD SELFESTEEM

Self-confidence and self-esteem are concepts of a psychological nature that greatly influence when meeting new people.

When what we are also looking for is to have an entertaining conversation with someone but to flirt, these two aspects' relevance is even greater. Here we will see some key ideas to know how to comment on them in this area of life.

Self-confidence and self-esteem in its expression when seducing

It would be a disagreement to think that people who have problems acting with confidence when flirting suffer this problem because they have low selfesteem or because they do not believe in themselves in a global sense. It is very common to meet people who generally trust their abilities in contexts that they face almost every day, such as studies or work, but who at the same time falter when they show self-confidence in specific situations they face. They confront each other in less systematic ways, such as when trying to flirt on weekends.

And it is that self-esteem and self-confidence are not completely homogeneous elements. Still, they have several facets and can change depending on the situation to which we are exposed. Many shy people are confident when speaking in front of an audience about a topic that fascinates them and they know well. Simultaneously, those who are usually popular can become insecure and vulnerable if they have to speak in front of the public about something they do not know well.

This means that to enhance our fluency in one area of social life, we must work in that area and not in any other.

Thus, the fundamental thing is to develop self-confidence and behavior patterns that promote self-esteem, specifically in seduction for the present case. Of course, working on self-esteem in a global sense, in the face of life as a whole, is important and contributes to making social interactions normally more fluid and enjoyable.

However, we should not stop at that, which can be used as an excuse for not having to "leave the comfort zone" and start developing communication skills based on meeting people and, why not, also seduction. Given that these types of challenges occur specifically in social interaction overcoming them must also focus on this type of social experience and not on others. In other words, the keys to developing self-confidence and self-esteem should be linked to the act of breaking the ice, showing interest, asserting yourself to people we don't know, and, in general, flirting. Let's see several ideas about it.

Four communicative keys to express seductive self-confidence when flirting These are several fundamental psychological keys that you must consider to gain ease and confidence when flirting.

# THE FEAR OF REJECTION IS BASED ON AN ILLUSION

This does not mean that the fear of rejection does not exist; On the contrary, it is a very real phenomenon and whose appearance (to a greater or lesser degree of intensity) is not rare, even in people who are better at flirting. The point is that on the one hand, as we have seen, we must not fight to eliminate the fear of rejection from our mind, and on the other, it must be clear that it is not based on facts that can reveal very unvarnished truths. Uncomfortable about who we are.

The fear of rejection has to do with anticipating the distressing implications of someone showing disinterest in us. This can very well happen: there are no reasons to assume that everyone finds us fascinating. But does this say something very bad about our identity? If they reject us, we seek to bring positions closer because they don't know us well in the vast preponderance of cases.

On the other hand, hardly a single interaction or series of a few interactions with someone will give us a realistic reflection on who we are. Self-concept, our idea of "I," is built over time and through hundreds of experiences. Having someone say "yes" or "no" at a point in the conversation is not going to break the schemes from which we analyze who we are, as frustrating as it can sometimes be.

# WITHOUT PRACTICE, THERE IS NO PROGRESS

Finally, knowing all of the above is of little use if it is not put into practice. To develop the social and emotional management skills necessary to flirt, you have to apply them to reality. For this reason, many people go to the psychologist to obtain the theory and a series of guidelines to commit to this process of change and use it effectively and avoid unnecessary frustrations, starting with what works for "beginners" and ending for the most ambitious challenges.

# TRUST IS THE KEY TO ATTRACTING WOMEN

Have you ever tried to begin a dialogue with a wonderful woman, only to find yourself drowning in your own words and stuttering like a maniac?

There is something about the image of meeting an attractive woman that turns men into jellyfish, but if you can overcome this fear and learn to be confident with women, you will look much more attractive.

If you're not feeling confident, show confidence anyway. In other words, pretend until you do.

It's not simple, but if you work hard to maintain strong body language and to keep your words in check, you will gradually begin to feel the confidence that you only intended to have at first. Remember, practice makes perfect. And while we're on the point of practice, you must put yourself in place to be around attractive women as much as possible.

If you find it challenging to stay calm with pretty girls, visit strip clubs, hostess bars, modeling events, and anywhere you know, attractive women will be in abundance.

Don't try to get involved with some of these women; hang out and have fun joking around. By regularly placing yourself in these settings and forcing yourself to interact with them, beautiful women will lose their charisma. It will be much more relaxed for you to communicate with them in any setting.

Also, sign up for dance or yoga classes. You will meet many women on these sites, and you can have fun just interacting and having fun with them. And as a bonus, women associate sexuality with men who can dance, so it's a situation you have nowhere to lose.

Last, and perhaps most important, erase the thought of outcome dependency from your mind. By not worrying about the result, you relieve yourself of the pressure, and it becomes easier to have fun and do your best.

Treat beautiful women exactly as you would any other girl, and stick to your original game plan, no matter how much you are tempted to revert to your old habits.
I always have a positive attitude, and it is the first step to achieve success with women. Therefore you must make an internal change in yourself.

If you thought you would get a girl's attention by playing the victim, you would only achieve her pity. Therefore, it is recommended that you show yourself happy, positive and show that being by your side is the greatest thing to happen to her.

It shows security, and it happens to many men that they feel a little intimidated by women since they are afraid of failure or making a fool of themselves.

Therefore, to achieve success, you must put aside fears, anxieties, and nerves and just be yourself.

There is no magic secret to being confident with women. Like everything, it's just a matter of changing your mindset.

# CONFIDENCE ATTRACTS WOMEN, DISCOVER HOW TO SHOW CONFIDENCE

Showing confidence is easy for many men when they are with other men, but the game changes when they are in front of a girl they like, sadly. So don't be surprised if you feel nervous or insecure when talking to a girl you like. Nevertheless, you should know that trust is the first thing you should develop if you are interested in seducing her. While gaining confidence can be difficult, you can at least pretend you have it and get it to notice you.

**Go straight to the point**

Some men fail to express themselves well when in front of a woman they like. As a consequence of this, they end up over-explaining to you. If you want the female of your dreams to be attracted to you, you must not allow nerves and fear to eat you up. Instead of hinting that she knows you want to ask her out, tell her that you want to ask her out. Instead of asking indirect questions in the hope of getting the answer to the question currently in your head, ask the question. In this way, you will avoid looking like a lost child, and you will finally have the necessary answer.

**Show your softer side**

Don't be scared to show a little emotion. Women respond well to men who can express some emotion. To work, you need to show your true feelings and share with her things that you are genuinely passionate about. Once she discovers that you can value the things that excite you, she will appreciate you much more. However, avoid losing your appeal easily when it starts to lead to the wrong things. If you start to get emotional in negative terms, she will think that there is something wrong with you and immediately walk away.

# DO NOT ASK FOR THEIR APPROVAL

Nothing shows less confidence in a man than feeling the need for constant compliments. Allow yourself to earn the compliments and handle your reactions correctly. If she offers you a compliment, politely thank her and tell her that you appreciate her for noticing. This will make her see that you are a man who has confidence in himself and does not need anyone's approval. Which by itself will help you appear much more attractive and will make him fall head over heels in love with you.

The truth is, if you show enough confidence, you won't even need to try too hard to attract any woman you want. So start practicing these tips right now and make her feel attracted to you almost instantly.

# THE BODY LANGUAGE

## What Is Communication?

It is worth questioning what it is about communication? There are many definitions of this word, but if we look at the Royal Spanish Academy, we will see that we mean "Transmission of signals through a common code to the sender and receiver" by communication. That is, in general terms that two or more people get to understand each other. It is simple, and we are talking about the elements that intervene in every communication process: Sender, message, channel, receiver, and code. Often it seems that the common code par excellence (which allows the sender to spread a message and the receiver to interpret it) is the word, the language, but it is not always the safest.

Once it has been defined that verbal communication is not the only method used to communicate, it is important to make clear, on the one hand, the relationship of interdependence that exists between the verbal and non-verbal channels (since they are not independent of each other, rather they complement each other ); and secondly, the contradictory nature of this relationship, since words can say something and gestures deny it.

# NON-VERBAL COMMUNICATION

When we talk about non-verbal communication, we refer to all those messages that we send without speaking. We talk about gestures, expressions, body movements, eye contact ... a whole series of signals that are very important in the relationship between people. Therefore, studying non-verbal communication means knowing how to interpret everything that words do not say.

If there are three important points to highlight about non-verbal communication, it is an unconscious type of communication that we cannot act on. Second, each gesture has meaning within the same context. Therefore, isolated gestures should not be analyzed but rather should be analyzed as a whole. And thirdly ... that human communication is very complex.

It should be remarked that non-verbal communication studies are relatively new. Although Darwin already pointed out some aspects of this science, until the beginning of the 20th century, there was no significant interest in communication through facial expressions.

Moreover, it took the 1950s for some authors to decide to channel the issue.

As Flora Davis points out, "Words are beautiful, fascinating and important, but we have overestimated them excessively" since, in communication, not all the merit of the message goes to the words. Still, there are a whole series of elements that also are present. Psychologist Albert Mehrabian decomposed the impact of a message in percentages, giving a first and important place to body language with 55%, a 38% to voice, and the last place to words with only 7%. These numbers, known as the 7% -38% -55% rule, do not apply to any communicative situation, they vary according to the circumstances, and on numerous occasions, the author denies their universal nature. As can be read on their website: "Total result = 7 Verbal + 38% Vocal + 55% Facial: Please note that this and other equations concerning the relative importance of verbal and non-verbal messages were derived from experiments related to communication of emotions and attitudes (i.e., like-dislike). Unless a communicator is speaking about their feelings or attitudes, these equations are not applicable. "

Once non-verbal communication is well defined, it is important to know how to distinguish the three typologies: Paralinguistic, Proxemic, and Kinesic.

Paralanguage is the set of non-verbal elements of the voice. We refer to its intensity or volume, speed, rhythm, intonation, laughter, and crying to understand each other better. For example, a deep voice will give us more respect and authority than a voice with low dominance.

Proxemics refers to the use of space by two or more people in the communication process. That is the distance between the emitter and the receiver. Edward T. Hall was a pioneer in researching the use of space. They speak of different types of distance:

- Public distance (more than 360 cm). Distance to speak in a group.
- Social distance (between 120 and 360 cm). Social gatherings and parties.
- Personal distance (between 46 and 120 cm). It is the distance that separates us from strangers.
- Close distance (between 15 and 45 cm). It is the most important and is what a person has as their own space. Only people with a very effective relationship are allowed to join.

Finally, Kinesic or Kinesis studies the meaning of body movements and gestures in a communicative situation ... It is essential to highlight that the body movements carried out may or may not have the intention and that eye movement is also included in Kinesic. Since this type of non-verbal communication is the one that can be seen represented in the short film, we will try to define it in greater detail. Kinesis types:

- **Posture:** It expresses the attitude of people concerning their environment. A distinction is made between an open posture, when a person opens up to communication without putting up physical barriers such as crossing arms or legs, and a closed position, when we cross arms and legs, separating ourselves from our interlocutor.

- **Gestures:** These are movements of any part of the body that can express a multitude of sensations and emotions. For example, showing the fist with the thumb raised will mean the familiar "OK."

- **Face expressions:** Through the face, we express countless states of mind; we can express up to 1000 possible emotions. In his book Emotion in the human Faces, Paul Ekman shows that facial gestures reflect our emotions. After many years of study, he established seven facial expressions on the human face: happiness, sadness, anger, disgust, surprise, fear, contempt.

- **The gaze:** Eye contact is very important since in the communicative act it plays a series of roles: it regulates communication (it is an indicator of the turn to speak or act), it is a source of information (a sustained gaze is not the same threatening than an affective look), expresses emotions and communicates the nature of the interpersonal relationship.

- **The smile:** It expresses joy, sympathy, or happiness. In his work Social Intelligence, Daniel Goleman writes, "Ekman has identified eighteen different types of smiles based on different combinations of the fifteen facial muscles involved." Among them, it is worth mentioning, to name just a few, the fake smile that seems attached to an unhappy face and transmits an attitude of the type "smile and cheer," which seems the very reflection of resignation; the cruel smile displayed by the wicked person who enjoys hurting others and the distant smile characteristic of Charles Chaplin, which mobilizes a muscle that most people cannot voluntarily move and seems, laugh out loud.

- **Touch and smell:** Human beings also communicate through smell and touch. Both the skin and the nose are receptors for messages.

# SEDUCTION

The cinema, television, literature, and theater have been in charge during all this time to remind us of great seducers who have marked history. Cleopatra, Casanova, Kenedy are just some of them.

Now let's take as a reference the meanings that the Royal Spanish Academy offers us about the word "seduction": Deceive with art and skill; Gently persuade for something bad. Physically attracting someone to obtain sexual intercourse from them and Seizing or captivating the mood.

It should be remarked that although most of the time we use this term to refer to sensual relationships, it is true that this is not the case since we can feel seduced by objects such as clothes or shoes, by the speech of a politician ... It is important to distinguish between affective, social and professional Seduction among others. For this reason, seducing is attracting or pleasing by physical appearance or an opinion. It is about offering something pleasant to the eye of our interlocutor. Argues the Psychologist Vallejo-Nájera, "We love that they seduce us because they are mainly offering us pleasure."

The psychologist affirms that "Seduction is related to love success, but it is not only that. We seduce each time we communicate, and we make the person in front of us feel attracted to us. There is a genetic load because more people are extroverts, who have it easier, and others less. But it also influences how we were the first relationships with parents, friends, teachers. "Therefore, Seduction does not only exist outside the love field, but we also seduce since we are little.

Vallejo-Nájera in Psychology of Seduction offers a classification of the existing seductive prototypes according to roles. He maintains that the first step is to discover which typology suits our characteristics.

● **Aphrodite:** Gives off sensuality, which offers serious, protective men. You want security and to feel pampered. His emotionality fluctuates between laughing and crying. The seductress feels that his image of a sexually powerful man is strengthened. To seduce her, you must offer her loyalty, security, and optimism.

● **The low life:** He seeks adventure and offers an overflowing passion to women who are a little insecure and maternal. For this, he entertains them with ardor. He is narcissistic but with self-esteem problems; therefore, he needs admiration. To win him over, you have to admire him and help him channel his emotions.

● **The rescuer:** It is the angel who solves all problems, offering help and generosity. They look for chaotic, clueless people with low self-esteem. He is motivated by feeling indispensable. To seduce them, you have to admire their help and help you to spend time with yourself.

- **The artist:** Creative and romantic, he looks for people who are sensitive to beauty, who are struck by his genius. They want to feel special, and therefore their idealism must be respected, valuing their authenticity.

- **The captivator:** Cheerful and agile verb, he is the king of empathy who looks for rigid and self-demanding people who need positivism. Enjoy life and to conquer him, you have to avoid being unhappy and not criticize anyone.

- **The intellectual:** Offers wisdom to anyone who wants intellectual stimulation. They are very selective and imply that they do not need the other. To conquer them, you have to respect their space and solitude and not overwhelm them with emotional demands.

- **The charming:** The oasis of tranquility and friendliness, support, and lack of pretense, especially with stress problems. The charmer does not argue and nurtures the opponent's self-esteem. It motivates you to feel comfortable.

- **The divo:** It is the style, the 'glamor' without apparent effort, with which he catches people overwhelmed by routine. The divo is ethereal, insinuating, and distant and seeks perfection. To attract him, you have to encourage him not to treat himself so harshly, to make him enjoy the small pleasures of an imperfect life.

# THE LANGUAGE OF SEDUCTION

"To be seductive. We all secretly dream of it, and we all defend ourselves well from its attacks; it is the nature of Seduction (...) The truth is that everyone wants to seduce, and Seduction is at the center of all human relationships" Philippe Turchet, The language of Seduction.

We will start from a premise: The most seductive people, beyond their physical appearance, are those who know how to communicate. There may be beautiful people who do not have Seduction's art among their gifts, who do not have that charm that captivates their interlocutors. Thus the words communication and Seduction are two processes that go hand in hand.

Logically before a good communicator, we are captivated, but not by the message sent, but by how it is transmitted. The seducing art is based on sending imperceptible messages (some messages only last hundreds of milliseconds) to make our listener interested. However, these messages are not indistinguishable to the brain, which is in charge of processing and adapting to them. Thus, it can be said that gestures act as subliminal messages.

Philippe Turchet, who in his book The Language of Seduction advises fleeing from words to seduce, is the father of Synology. This science was born in the 1980s after several years of study. This discipline tries to decipher the meaning of small gestural details, facial micro-expressions, gestures, and body movements that we perform unconsciously (such as why we support our head on one of our hands or why we cross our legs).

We have already commented that words should not be as important as gestures in the communication process; that is why we must give a vote of confidence to gestures in the event of a contradiction between gestures and words. Many studies show that words are unable to convey emotions.

A very decisive stage in Seduction is childhood. Although it may not appear similar to it, this process does not develop when we reach a certain age, but since we are small and we make contact with social relationships, we learn to use it. We have always seen how there are children at school who are more charismatic than others.

## Head and face

When it comes to representing emotions on the face, various elements act the mouth, the eyebrows, the eyes, and the gaze.

It should be noted that the left part of the face is the part of the emotions, controlled by the right hemisphere. However, the right part is the control part and is directed by the left hemisphere. Very contrary to what we think, our face is not symmetrical.

## The eyes and the gaze

If we observe our interlocutor's gaze, we can answer some questions, such as if they pay attention to us or simply if we attract them. In this sense, the eyelids play a fundamental role, since when people are listening, we weblink to accept the information that comes from outside. A person who stops blinking does not pay attention. Like when we use the expression "Being in Babia" to describe someone clueless. The more I blink, the more immersed you are in the conversation.

Another detail to highlight is the brightness of the eyes or the size of the pupils. When we are in the appearance of someone we love, our eyes become moist, and the pupils tend to increase in size. Simultaneously, if our interlocutor looks at us, and the desire is mutual, his pupils will also enlarge.

## The eyebrows

When we worry that our interlocutor does not open up to communication, our eyebrows immediately take a "V" shape. This gesture will show on your face that something is not right for many words that say otherwise.

## The mouth

This part of the face is considered a very desirable area. Logically, the actions we perform with our mouths are different from what we can perform with our eyes. If we realize, when we are interested in a person, our gaze goes directly to his mouth. It is a form of approximation. Besides, we also use our mouth to moisten our lower lip, thus expressing our desire. If this movement is made from left to right, the desire is sexual.

## The smile

To know if a smile has been sincere, it is enough to analyze if the eyebrows have descended, wrinkles have been created on the crow's feet, and if the teeth are visible. If this does not happen, the smile is fake.

## The hand on the face

When our hands go to the face, it is not by chance; they also intend to transmit messages. A well-known sign covers your mouth with your hands, which is nothing more than an expression of shame derived from childhood when we hide our faces behind our palms.

Another well-known sign that creates a lot of controversies is that of stroking your hair with your hands. It is thought that this act is a sign of Seduction, but it is not like that; not all hand gestures with hair have that intention. Some are only self-contact, while others are looking for an approximation. To know how to distinguish, it is important to look at how high the hand is, if it is close to the listener or if, on the contrary, it is as far away as possible. Besides, the palm state also comes into play; if it is uncovered, it expresses opening, while if the person making the gesture is hidden, it closes.

Another very common gesture is to support the head; on the one hand, this gesture is nothing more than the desire to attract attention, to seek that our interlocutor looks at us. **Micro-itches**

A distinction must be made between itching that appears because we are uncomfortable and itching that is sexual. When we talk about the former, we refer to situations in which we are with someone we like, but for some reason, we are uncomfortable, and our body reacts through itching in the ear, nose, chin, or cheek. Regarding the latter, the most important is the one that appears in the "Cupid's Bow," the space between the higher lip and the nose.

## The gestures

Gestures in conversations are more than important. Rather than complement the word, they provide the true meaning of the message. Some studies show that Italians are the most seductive people in Europe. Coincidentally they are the ones who have the most gestures in their culture.

## The hands

The hands say a lot about our emotions. If we present the open palm when we speak, this translates into an opening to communication; the opposite occurs when the palms are not shown. If we hide them, for example, behind our back, we are hiding our emotions. Also, when we decide not to participate in communication, our hands lower their temperature.

## The shoulders

This area is very special since next to the neck, we reserve it for very effective relationships. By caressing some part of the body, we unconsciously take our interlocutor to the area where the caresses fall. If a man and a woman are attracted at high levels, they make small movements with the left shoulder as a call.

## The trunk

The trunk is faithfully linked to our ego, to our person. If you think about it, when we refer to ourselves, we touch the trunk. In this area, a series of trunks may appear, especially in the left breast. This action represents contradictory wishes. When, for example, we want to get close to someone, but something holds us back.

## Arms and forearms

Together with the hands, the arms and the forearms are an extension of what we say; they also symbolize people's relationships. When we caress our arms on the outside, we are expressing the desire to be caressed. It is very important to see how the fists are because if they are not supinated, we want to be caressed, but we do not open ourselves, especially to the person close to us. This gesture is deepened if a slight tilt of the head accompanies it. Another common gesture is crossing your arms and stroking your shoulder with one hand. If we caress the right shoulder, our feelings are closed; however, our emotions are externalized if we caress the left shoulder.

If what is caressed is the forearm, this gesture indicates a desire to be closer to the interlocutor. We offer ourselves to them; we are more distant from the trunk, from our person. Besides, the caresses in the inner part of this area indicate a relational desire.

When there are contradictory thoughts about a couple's desire, our body also reacts with slight itching in these areas as repression. These micropores represent a contradiction between what is said and what is thought, between words and emotions.

**Fingers**

The heart and the ring finger are two fingers that play an important role in the seductive process. The middle finger represents a physical desire, while the ring finger is the symbol of union. If a person wears a ring between their fingers and slides it all over their finger, it means they want to get closer. It does not have to be a sexual desire since, between friends, it can happen.

**Elbows and wrists**

Elbows are very present in desire; we use them to give hugs. Micro-itches may appear on the elbow; this gesture denotes a large opening.

On the other hand, when we talk and gesture, our wrists' state is of special importance. If we open them, presenting them, we offer ourselves to communication. However, if we hide them, we are expressing a rejection.

**The legs**

Just as the upper part of the body expresses affective desires, the lower part symbolizes physical desires, so both parts' messages are different. It should be noted that with the legs, we have much greater freedom of movement than with the arms. Besides, there are situations in which the legs are subject to being hidden (when we are sitting at a table), but this does not mean that they do not express their desire but rather express themselves with greater autonomy. Leg crosses serve to exclude and include people in a specific situation. Just look at which leg we cross and where the leg is pointing to know who we are leaning towards.

Another difference between the two parts of the body is that men do not use the lower part in the same way as women to express openness. First, the females open their ankles or, if they are sitting, make slight movements with the ankle that will point the interlocutor. However, males slightly spread their legs. Also, if they scratch their knee, they express the desire to get close to a woman. If what they scratch is the thigh, they manifest sexual desire.

# WHAT IS BODY LANGUAGE?

The communication that we carry out through our body greatly influences social relationships and is the perfect mirror of emotions.

It has happened to everyone that they have met a person, but this person did not convey confidence. This is frequently because there is a contradiction between what they are communicating verbally and their body language.

**Body language:** It is a kind of non-verbal communication based on the gestures, poses, and movements of the body and face. It is usually done automatically, so it is a good indicator of the person's emotional state.

On other occasions, the opposite may happen, that we meet someone who has coordinated body language and verbal communication and gives us good feelings. There are many moments in the business world when you have to speak in public and generally under pressure, so you must have good control over non-verbal language. This way, you will be closer to achieving your goal. The examples that you can see in this post will be great for:

- Presentations
- Talks.

- Network.

Of course, you must mind that non-verbal communication can be influenced by environmental circumstances, and, therefore, it is not an arbitrary truth. To be able to do an inspection and be sure of it, you must find periodic signals.

# HOW TO IMPROVE YOUR BODY LANGUAGE

Body language is ancient and innate to us; it is even more so than the language itself and facial expressions. That is why blind people make the same body language expressions as people who can see. It comes as preprogrammed in our brain.

I have always been fascinated with this and how it helps us achieve our goals in life. The power of body language is described very well by Amy Cuddy in her famous phrase:

*"Our non-verbal*
*language governs the*
*way other people think*
*and feel about us."*

If you're anything like me, then you've had a healthy obsession with this for some time. Some studies at Harvard, Princeton, and other major universities have shared something new on this topic and how to use it at work in recent years. Although the power of communication is very important in delivering the right message, the power of body language can be a determining factor in how someone makes us feel.

Here is a sampling of some of the studies on how to use non-verbal language to your advantage every day:

Your body expressions express more emotion than your face. We all turn up discovering how to deal with others based on facial expressions. Nevertheless, that may not be the best way to judge someone else's emotions. Researchers at Princeton did a simple experiment. They asked study participants to judge a photograph if they felt happiness, loss, victory, or pain. Some photos simply showed facial expressions, some body language, and some both.

In four experiments, participants guessed emotion based on body language alone or combined with facial expressions - rather than easy expression alone. Extremely negative or extremely positive emotions are especially difficult to distinguish.

Body language is not something we have to learn. Most of the emotional expressions already come into our system. For example, scientists in British Columbia observed people with congenital blindness at the Paralympic Games. So if body language is so ancient and so powerful in expressing our true emotions, how can we best use it in our lives to achieve what we want?

# BODY LANGUAGE CHANGES US

Amy Cuddy describes some of the most peculiar events of body language. It focuses on the business world and how non-verbal language is good for this, and the possibilities seem limitless. Cuddy chooses between two different types of body postures. One is the pose of power, and the other is the one that has no power.

Cuddy's research reveals a lot of interesting things. The first tells us that expressing more power poses helps us get jobs, makes us feel better and more successful.

You don't have to do much, just improve the position of your arms or legs. Cuddy explains that there will also be changes in our body when there are changes in our body language. These changes have to do with hormones:

- Testosterone. The "power" hormone, where among other things, it helps us to be better leaders, have more focus and attention.
- Cortisone. The "stress" hormone, which, among other things, makes us less reactive to stress, distresses us, and we feel powerless.

The key is to fake it until you believe it. Here are five poses to work on today to answer the question, "How can I improve my body language?"

**Focus on the status of your feet.**

Carol Kinsey Goman has examined the importance of body language in the workplace for many years. One of his best tips is to pay attention to your feet.

Many times we focus on the top, but the feet reveal more about our emotions than we would like to think:

"When you approach two people talking, you can be perceived in one of two styles. If your two colleagues' feet stay in place and twist only their upper torso in your direction, they don't want to join your conversation. But if their feet open to including, you know you are invited to participate. "

To find out if the conversations are over, she advises us this: "When you're talking to a co-worker who appears to be paying attention and whose top is tilted toward you, but their legs and feet are facing the door, the conversation is over. His feet are telling you that he wants to leave. The position of the feet can be revealed even if the legs are crossed. "

**Smile; it will make you happier.**

We smile because we are right, but does it work the other way?

Researchers at Cardiff University think so. Without actually feeling happy, people who laugh can make them even happier, says Michael Lewis, a coauthor of the study.

"It seems that the way we feel about our emotions does not depend only on our brain; there are parts of our body that help reinforce the feelings we are having."

Being able to smile well is another story. For now, try smiling in the bathroom or another quiet place before a difficult conversation, job interview, or meeting. It will make you feel more triumphant.

**Practice Amy Cuddy's "power poses" before critical meetings.**

Practice three different power poses for 2 - 3 minutes before having an extensive interview.

Try them next time in a peaceful place and see if you get the same results.

# REALIGN YOUR BODY WHEN YOU HAVE A CONVERSATION

Another tip of Goma is that if you try to change your position when having a chat, you will reduce the tension in conversations and develop faster solutions.

"If you physically align yourself with these people (standing, sitting shoulder to shoulder in the same direction), you can defuse the situation."

**Lower your voice by breathing deeply.**

Although this is not a specific type for body posture, it is one of my favorites. Men and women with more deep voices are more likely to rise to leadership positions and are perceived as an authority.

To lower your voice, especially before an interview, try taking a few deep breaths. It will relax your throat, which generally contracts and raises the pitch of your voice.

Body language is much more important than we often think. It is so important that, according to multiple studies, about 93% of what we transmit in a conversation is non-verbal communication.

# WHAT SHOULD YOU LOOK FOR IN YOUR PARTNER'S BODY LANGUAGE?

Below you will see different non-verbal language techniques and what their meanings may be:

non-verbal language Meaning of facial gestures in non-verbal language When we speak, we see the person in front of us, so eye contact with the other person's face is almost obligatory and continuous. Many elements such as eyes, smiles, or hands brought to the face have much more meaning than we think.

**Pupil size**

It is one of the great acquaintances within body language. The decrease can mean dislike for what is being seen, while the increase means pleasure. This effect is often invisible because the pupils also adapt to changes in the environment.

**Eye contact**

To a considerable extent, this factor depends on the person who receives it and, therefore, within non-verbal communication, and it can have a positive or negative interpretation. It depends on the awareness that the reaction is produced in the person. **Prolonged eye contact**

Staring into a person's eyes for a long period can mean that you lie to that person. In this way, he keeps his gaze, sometimes without blinking, to dodge being discovered in the deception.

**Look sideways**

It is an action that can have an unenthusiastic meaning since, in non-verbal language, it means indifference and that you are looking for escape routes to distract yourself.

**Touch your nose**

It is different from the great acquaintances in body language. The main meaning is that the person making the gesture is lying, but sometimes it can mean that the person is offended or shocked.

**Voice tone and volume**

Are one of the essential elements in non-verbal language.

As a clarification, it must be said that the tone is the timbre of the voice, while the volume is the power of it.

# CROSSED LEGS

It is a defensive and closed attitude. When a person chooses this posture with arms and legs crossed in a social context, they are not immersed in the conversation. In a marketing context, it means that the person is closed mentally, emotionally, and actually.

**Crossed ankles**

This sign is still within protective body language, just like when we cross our legs. This gesture is made to maintain control.

**Hiding behind someone or something**

When a person is speaking, either standing or sitting and puts an objective between himself and the person or persons he is speaking, he seeks to defend himself. This shows that you are not sure what you are saying and are afraid to say it if it fails.

**Expansive stance**

When we converse, our feet are separated (at the height of the shoulders), and the arms are slightly open showing the palms. In this way, there is a posture of honesty and of not hiding anything with which you gain trust among the public.

# IMITATE LANGUAGE

When you're speaking to someone you like, the positions and movements are related. This way, you can determine if the talks or meetings are going as intended.

If the person you are talking to follows your movements and postures, the conversation goes very well.

**Jug pose**

It is a posture that affords greater presence and power. It happens when your feet are at shoulder height and your hands are on your hips. In this position, the chest's position also intervenes; the more outside it is, the more aggressive it will communicate.

## Stick out breast

This posture occurs when the person feels they have power and control. This is very important as it means that the person has achieved some accomplishment of which they are proud. In postures to increase superiority, it can also communicate aggressiveness,

*Change your body language to improve your communication skills.*

Body language speaks for us; that is why it is one of the others' most important aspects. At work, mastering body language is also essential to communicate properly and demonstrate your ability.

Interpretations of body language can be misleading. As Ginny Soskey tells us on HubSpot Blogs, "If you want others to understand what you want to say without confusion, you must ensure that your facial expression, your posture, and other non-verbal signals are in tune with your message."

A person is capable of generating 250,000 different facial expressions and more than 1,000 different body postures. 82% of messages enter us through the eyes, compared to 11% that we perceive through the ear. It took us only 7 seconds to pass judgment on someone just after seeing them. Incredible true?

This is why there are such numerous body language features that influence our work's success or failure, and of course, in our daily negotiations. In addition to the five tips on body language that we gave you to improve your negotiations, take note of these recommendations to improve your communication skills and develop your leadership skills:

Have a positive attitude and maintain eye contact with the person you are addressing; nods from time to time and smiles. Stand up and take up space; This posture shows security and confidence and is the way to establish power if you act from a leadership position. Coordinate your body language with your verbal message; avoid contradictions. Keep a correct physical distance with the person or group with whom you speak. Not too close to be aggressive, not too far to suggest contempt or indifference.

Let others talk, don't interrupt, and pay attention. Avoid distracting gestures (for example, looking at your nails or clothes). If you are forced to disagree, use your body language to support your position. Make proper physical contact without being threatening. Do not turn your back on others. Adopt a kind posture that inspires confidence and sincerity. Do not be afraid to gesticulate while you speak; it has been proven that following a piece of information with gestures serves to understand the information better because the words become visible to our understanding.

Mastering body language is part of the difficulty of developing communication skills, which are increasingly sought after in the business world, even above employees' technical knowledge. That is why it is important to work on our soft skills with Merchants and Triskelion programs for our individual and professional growth.

# BODY LANGUAGE AS A WEAPON OF SEDUCTION

The body allows you to seduce without a word. If you are one of those who, when you speak, the bread rises, it is better that you use body language to flirt.
All human beings can flirt using body language. There are several infallible techniques to achieve the purpose successfully. Men and women use different gestures to take their flirt to the garden, but how should we use non-verbal language as a Seduction weapon?

**They: a movie hunk**

Before starting to forge the strategy, the man must put himself in the woman's shoes and know what is expected in that meeting: discard the idea of talking, thinking, or looking at other women. She and nothing but her is the target.

She stares into hers as if there is no tomorrow: knowing how to look is almost as important as knowing how to speak. Through the look, a person will give more or less confidence to repeat a second date. When someone looks at you, it is because they are interested in you, in your conversation, and your experiences. Don't get lost!

Take charge of the date: women like to control the situation but at the same time feel controlled. Taking the reins means keeping the thread of the conversation, bringing up topics, choosing the menu, and of course, paying the bill. Be careful going from controlling the situation to trying to control the girl!

**Hands-on the table:**

You don't have to be too smart; some girls like a touch, but others don't even like the sound of the wind on the first date. Use your hands to emphasize conversations, touch your chin or just have it because of your flirt. A large, well-groomed hand says a lot about the type of man in front of it.

# DON'T BE RUDE:

Girls who like bad men are an old-fashioned myth. Now what is carried are the men who put themselves in women's shoes, listening and sharing. Attentive! Do not fall into being too cakey because you will bore the girl, and she will run away. He wants to take her to bed, not be her best friend.

The half-smile is better than the laugh: if the situation turns out to be funny, it is always a point in your favor. The best option to be funny without being rude is not to go overboard with the laugh or the easy (or macho) joke. On the one hand, you will be fatal, and on the other, you can be offended. A halfsmile is always much sexier and more manly.

A picture is worth a thousand terms: it's true. Men who take care of themselves are increasingly liked, those who know how to choose their clothes well, and those who, despite their three-day beard, are perfectly shaved. Take care of your image. They are the alphabet letters of your body language.

# NON-VERBAL SIGNS THAT SCREAM "I'M NOT DOMINANT. "AND HOW TO AVOID IT!

What do you think makes a guy more attractive to girls? It is the impression that you are a dominant man, in a good way. And no, you don't have to snort, scratch, and slap women like a caveman to demonstrate dominance ... nor should you! You transport your dominant male state by simply acting in the way that dominant males do, consciously controlling the non-verbal signals they send out, thus creating an impression on the female that you are Alpha. This technique is called the association principle. Within a woman's mind, you associate yourself with desirable masculine traits while casting off the undesirable "good guy" traits.

This is how magicians act. On stage, the magician carefully controls the impression he makes on the audience. By diverting the audience's attention to things they associate with magic — like his wand — he prevents the audience from noticing the things that would make him appear non-magical: the fact that he is using his hand to do the trick! Similarly, you can use the direction of the impression to control what the woman thinks of you. And here's some really good news for you: by adopting the proper mindset discussed in this guide, you will eventually grow up to be a full alpha male. And you can start walking in that direction today by choosing the behavior of an alpha male.

So what is domination? It is the social control that comes from being successful. As you go through self-improvement, you will internalize the concepts in this book and become an alpha male in the future. Right now, learn to act like an alpha male, giving the impression of dominance using your voice, your eyes, your demeanor, and your posture.

Your gaze is the first non-verbal signal that tells people that you are an alpha male. A dominant man is not afraid to stare at people. By looking away, you communicate submission. When you look down, you communicate shyness, shame, and a sense of low status. When you're speaking, there is no boundary to how much eye contact you can perform. Studies have revealed that the more eye contact the speaker makes, the more dominant the person is perceived.

However, when you are the one listening, the opposite happens: the less you look at the other person speaking, the more dominant you become. (It has been wondered why adults say to children, "Look at me when I'm talking to you?" It is a way of reinforcing the adult's dominance over the child.) Of course, you do not want to be above the woman and think that you look at her from below. If you are perceived as too dominant, then start to suffer from her dislike. So give your eyes a break from time to time.

Another indicator of dominance is your voice. Assertive people control the dialogue. They also speak in a sarcastic voice and are not afraid to interrupt another person. Researches have shown that using a soft, quiet voice gives the impression that you are not assertive. When you converse, try to let your words run and not be afraid to say what's on your mind. People who hesitate and get stuck are perceived as less powerful than those who don't.

Look at their mannerisms and behaviors. Try to avoid the following nonverbal indicators of beta status:

**1)    Use "ah" and "um," partial sentences and incomplete words**. Studies have shown that people consider those who speak well to be lacking confidence and not very bright. It is a sign of nervousness. The reason we say "um" is because we are afraid of being interrupted by another person. Instead, don't be scared to pause for effect. Hesitating before important points will make you appear more competent, and people will remember what you say.

**2)     talking too fast**. This gives the impression that you are feeling anxious and have low self-confidence. A normal and comfortable conversation is in a moderate range of 125 to 150 words per minute. Slow down!

**3)     Speaking in a monotonous voice, also known as stuttering**. People with a narrow range of tone are seen as shy, uninteresting, and lacking in confidence. So vary its hue, and it will be perceived as an alpha.

**4)     Pausing too long before answering a question**. This indicates that you are overthinking his answer, which makes him seem indecisive. It will also appear that you are trying too hard to win the other person's approval.

**5)     Closed postures. An alpha spreads his arms and legs out and is open**. When standing, you can reinforce your body language by hooking your thumbs into your back pockets.

**6)     Keep your hands in front of you**. This is a defensive gesture. Instead, be open and vulnerable. (You are vulnerable because you are not afraid.) Let your arms relax and remain open. No one's going to hit him, so why does he need to crash?

**7)      Play with your fingers or hands**. When you are at the table in front of someone, there is a natural inclination to play with the sugar packets or wrappers with your fingers. Do not do it. And don't hit the table with your fingers - women hate that.

**8)      Touching her face while speaking**. This indicates that you are overthinking, indecisive, or shy. To confer confidence, hold your hands together in a needle shape in front of your chest or face. (Many teachers do this when they are lecturing.) Another pose that will help you when you need a great display of confidence is to hold their hands on their hips. Police officers do this when they need to establish authority over criminal suspects.

**9)      Bend or cross your arms in front of you**. On unique occasions, it is reasonable to fold your arms into an alpha shape (see Brad Pitt in Fight Club for a simple example of this), but as a general rule, avoid it.

**10)   Stiff or stooped posture**. An alpha male has a relaxed position, whether he is standing or sitting. Let go and relax.

**11)   downward gaze**. Alpha men hold their heads high. It is a show of enthusiasm, energy. Looking at the ground conveys the "loser" message. Lift your chin. Expose your neck — don't worry, no one is going to strangle you! Look at the person you are talking to; remember what I said about using your gaze.

**12)   Nervous facial gestures**. Such as licking, he was pursuing or biting lips, sharply pinching your nose. An alpha keeps a relaxed face and mouth because he is not afraid of anything or anyone.

**13)   smile excessively**. Primate studies have shown that beta males will smile more to signify their innocence to stronger males. Beta humans smile to show they are not a threat. The Alpha, however, only smiles when there is something to smile about. And yes — he can be a threat.

**14)   Walk briskly as part of your normal walk**. Instead, walk a little more gradually than normal, almost like you're bragging. You are Alpha — no one is chasing you, and you are not rushing to please anyone. If you're not in a rush to get somewhere, walk around as if you're relaxed and confident. Think: "I am the man. I can make any woman happy".

**15)   Walk only with your legs**. Don't be afraid to push your torso and arms. Try this: walk as you've just had incredible success and feel on top of the world. Watch what you do with your body. You may be moving your arms along with your shoulders and having a slight jump in your stride. Now, do it all the time.

**16)   Slack posture**. You don't have to put up with standing uncomfortably straight, but you do have to push your shoulders back. Watch Brad Pitt in any of his movies for examples of how to keep your back straight comfortably.

**17)   blink a lot**. Instead, blink slowly. Don't close your eyes awkwardly. Just allow your kids to relax. Let them drop a bit. Don't make insect eyes.

**18)   Alternate your eyes from side to side when speaking**. That is very beta. When you are in a conversation and are speaking, stare into the other person's face. Nonverbally, this communicates that you are saying something important and worth listening to.

**19)   Maintaining too much eye contact when the other person speaks**. Ignore the advice books that tell you to maintain continuous eye contact. The non-stop eye contact makes him seem needy, socially retarded, and frankly like a weirdo. Instead, allow your eyes to stray and then stare into her eyes. Look through it rather than at it. From extensive testing, I have found that staring at a woman about two-thirds of the time is optimal. By the way, just keep your gaze when she's saying something genuinely interesting to you. On the other hand, focus on another part such as your breasts, hair, things that happen around you, etc.

**20)    Uncomfortable eyes**. The bottom line is that your eyes should be happy, relaxed, assertive, and sexual.

**21)    Look down or to the side before answering a question from a woman**. If you need to look away before answering to think about the answer, look up and to the side. Studies have shown that this shows more confidence.

**22)    fear touching a woman**. Be safe and confident when touching a woman - any nervousness can be fatal to your relationships with her. Be Alpha and physically move it when you need it. Hold her hand to guide her, etc. Be gentle — if you use too much pressure, it reveals your insecurity. (Since you're Alpha, she's sure to follow, there's so no need to be anything other than playful and cuddly.) It's natural to touch other people, like when you're emphasizing a point. So let the love flow!

**23)    Quickly turn your head when someone wants your attention**. Instead, perform movements that you would do at home — slow and relaxed. You are not waiting for the call of others. You are the Alpha, don't forget.

**24)    Use long, twisted phrases**. Alphas keep the conversation short and get to the point. If you tend to use long sentences, separate them.

Don't feel bad if you inevitably slip and use one of these non-verbal cues from time to time. Nobody is perfect, lest he is hard on himself, especially when talking to a woman. Let it go and keep the conversation going.

When you think too much about such things that while speaking, you start to doubt, and when that happens, you feel vulnerable and afraid and start to hesitate. Instead, work on remaining indifferent and sincere at all times.

It is enough to easily be informed of how you communicate nonverbally through everything you do. Being aware means that you will start to avoid negative communication much more from now on.

# PRACTICING THE BODY LANGUAGE

Look at a man with high status - Brad Pitt, George Clooney, or the President of the company where you work - and you will notice that they move differently than the rest of us. They give off vibes that they are phenomenal, and for that reason, women squirt for them.

*You, too, can perform that aura that makes you beautiful to women.*

Have you ever regarded the way your friends look when they feel like shit? They stare at the ground with their arms crossed, their shoulders slumped and emitting other non-alpha behaviors.

Now think about the successful bastards. They bring all the old ladies around them, and some go around with motherly body language.

Here are a few points for body language (which, by the way, if you think it's easy, you're correct ... you can make these changes as fast as tonight and have the horniest old ladies clamoring for your attention.)

**1) relax**. This is the most remarkable state of mind you should be in.

**A) Do not feel worried**.
Let your worries go as you cannot solve any problem by worrying. So don't suck, and stop thinking about what's wrong. Just live the crazy life.

Now, I know that it is easier said than done (I used an old phrase, but relevant in this case). You have spent your entire life now emphasizing the thoughts that make you feel most worried.

But what is that emotion that we call "worry?" When you think about it, it is simply the fear of what might happen in the future. You are essentially punishing yourself by feeling upset before bad things happen. So there is no logical sense to worry!!

So pollution is avoiding your worrying thoughts at all costs. Identify them for what they are - toxic to your emotional states - and let them go.

Simply NOT emphasizing negative results that make you feel upset will reduce your worries by 90%.

**B)  Breathe through your abdomen, preferably of your chest**.

When you breathe, imagine that you are bringing air into your stomach. Feel your belly swell and deflate when you breathe.

**C)  Avoid non-verbal behaviors that are contrary to relaxation**:

+ Elevate your shoulders.

+ Wrinkle your forehead

+ Nervously moving
your hands or legs. +
Tighten your facial
muscles.

**D) Relax your muscles and slow down all your movements.**

Alpha males generally move slowly, as if in control of time. Beta males are nervous and make awkward movements. Imagine that you are standing and walking in a pool, where your movements are slow and fluid.

**E) Relax your eyes and your eyelids.**

Beta males keep their eyelids wide open because they are so nervous. His eyes flicker. Instead, let your eyelids rest. Look straight ahead. Only pay consideration to things if they interest you. While you are out and about, make the affirmation, "I am Sexual, I am Relaxed, I am in Control."

**F) If someone requires your attention, move your head slowly.**

A common trait among quite a few Beta males is, so eagerness to please that you see them turn their heads towards the other person strangely quickly when someone calls out to them.

# 2) FEEL MASCULINE ANDPOWERFUL

Visualize that you are a masculine man. Do the things in your life that make you feel manly, like lifting weights and exercising with a punching bag.
Watch your health.

# 3) Realize that you are a man of great value.

Focus on your classes and ignore your needs. To be completely confident, think things like, "I'm the mere dick, I'm a Chingón, everyone peels me."

Sound arrogant? See it as a therapy to overcome your lack of security. You will want to moderate yourself at some point once you have become successful and know that you are amazing (so that you don't act like an asshole), but until then, constantly think about your greatness.

Treat people as if they respect you even before you meet them. If you have to, visualize Elvis Presley: "Thank you, thank you very much ..."

# 4) Be comfortable in your skin.

An Alpha male is smiling with or without a particular female, as he regards women as the source of fun in his life - no more, no less. Take the attitude that, of course, women love you, but it's not a big deal either way.

# 5) Extend your body.

Take up your space with your arms, legs, and chest. Keep your neck aligned with your back so that your head is held high.

(Something that served me to get used to having my neck aligned was removing the pillow from my bed. After all, it is more challenging to have optimal posture when your neck is bent for 8 hours each night).

# SEDUCTION

Generally, women don't make things easy for you. She is rarely going to give you an obvious sign of her interest to move forward, to kiss her, or even if she likes you or just sees you as a 'friendly' man with whom she would spend some time chatting.

Keeping her interest can be very difficult; if you see the chemistry evaporate, the longer the conversation lasts. Besides, since she's not giving you a signal, it seems impossible to start touching or isolating her or doing whatever it is that lets her know that you are attracted to her and that you want to kiss her.

Even when I was with a girl on a date, I could not enjoy it because I felt anxious before the kiss, and I always thought about how I would transition to my move. I will give you my "Chemistry Test," a simple play that you can use to test if there is chemistry between the two of you. (Simple as it is, I've found it to be incredibly successful.)

Right now, since you don't know how to bring the interaction to a sexual level, you lose the girls; And when you make a mistake with a woman, she will rarely give you a second chance. The 3-Step System to Slow Down Into Sex, which I will teach you, will fix your problem of not knowing when to play it (or if you should even).

As you flirt (don't chat, flirt; there is a big difference), she will be doing things that encourage you to jump for the close; And without you even noticing what it is doing, it will make things easier for you.

I decided to create this chapter because most of the questions a man can have are related to this idea of taking a 'normal' conversation and making it a flirty, sexual interaction.

Men always want to know:

- How to excite a woman from the beginning?
- How do you get him to see you as a possible sexual partner?
- How do you let her comprehend that you are interested in her sexually?
- Since she feels like she's attracted to you, what do you do?
- What to do if you have little experience or are even a virgin and he beginsto ask you about your sexual life?

# Serious Mistakes You Probably Make That Keep Her From Your bedroom.

There tend to be certain serious mistakes that are somewhat common, and I see that men constantly make with their women.

The first mistake is this idea of pretending you don't care. I think this stems from men heeding suggestions like "don't look too interested" or "you have to be arrogant."

Shy men often fall into this trap because they use "disinterest" as an excuse to dodge placing themselves in a situation where they have to be proactive. I know because before I was very shy and girls rarely had any idea that I liked them. For my ego, it was good because I was rarely rejected. However, it was lousy for my sex life because I hardly ever slept with someone.

But there is an even bigger mistake that men make. The mistake is that they believe that the more they talk to a woman, and the better she likes them, the easier it will be to start flirting and being sexual with her.

The truth is that it is the other way around. The more you talk to a woman or get to know her without becoming sexual; it will be more likely that nothing will NEVER happen to her. The correlation is the opposite: the better a woman likes you, the less likely she is to be sexually attracted to you.

# THERE ARE THREE GENERAL RULES FOR TAKING ON A ROLE:

1. Take on the role from the beginning of the conversation
2. Own the role / be congruent
3. And know when to drop it

You want to exercise full control over the role you take on. From the beginning, you are more or less saying, "these are the rules for our conversation."This is very important, and you must establish the "role of your character" from the beginning. It will seem strange if you start practicing after 30 minutes of "normal" conversation. And then you must own the role and be congruent with it. This means you CAN'T back down if she gives you "shit tests." Don't wait for her to "support" the game you set; just jump right into it.

And finally, you need to know when to drop it. At some point, after the attraction has been created, there will come the point where the paper must be used in

MODERATION because if you never let go of the paper, she will never experience a deep sense of relationship WITH YOU.

How to take a position and use it immediately now in the real world ...

Okay.

Here's a character practice exercise:

Imagine a certain type of character you can work with ....

Choose one of these three:

1. An overconfident Playboy
2. She is a girl who demands a lot of attention
3. You are the Devil on his left shoulder (the Devil who orders him to do badthings)

Once you have selected one of the above characters, get in touch with how he could respond, react, what kind of facial expressions he would make, what would his tone of voice be like?

Spend a few minutes getting into the mind of the character you have chosen. Become him as you develop this exercise.

Your reactions come off the character.

Now how would an individual character answer the following three things?

1. She accidentally touches your leg

2. She drops something

3. She invites you to order her a drink

Her: (Accidentally touching your leg) So what are you working on?

A lady who requires a lot of attention: Oh my god! How dare you touch my leg? I'm not the boy you think I am ... With me, you're not going to get what you want just by sweetening my ear ...

Her: (Casually touching your ass) So what do you work on?

You are the Devil on her left shoulder - (the Devil who orders her to do bad things): Just ... slowly ... put ... your hand back on his butt ... She won't notice ... do it ... meanwhile, bend over and show her something of your chest ...

More examples ...

Her: (drops her cell phone)

Overconfident Playboy: You're taking every opportunity to show me your belongings ... right sweetheart? I admit it ... I enjoy the effort you're settling into this whole seduction thing ... most girls don't try that hard ...

Her: (drops her cell phone)

A lady who requires a lot of attention: Oh, please ... DON'T THINK you're going to cheat on me ... you just want me to look at your ass ... I'm not that kind of man.

Her: (drops her cell phone)

You are the Devil on his left shoulder - (the Devil who orders him to do bad things): He's watching ... Just lean a bit more ... maybe pull your hair back a bit ... and then make a stupid statement about "how drunk you are ..." Can you see how taking on the role of a character adds a more interesting touch to everything? ... And also allows you to introduce Sexy Themes Do you see how easy it is to transform the atmosphere of a short talk completely? And can you understand how EASY it is ALWAYS to KNOW WHAT TO SAY when you're performing a "role?" You just say what you believe your character would say

Just to illustrate the difference ... use one of the examples above (Her dropping her phone or touching your leg) and imagine how you would have acknowledged if it had been simply YOU (without assuming the role of any character) ...

You probably would have answered his stupid question, "what do you work on?" and carry on through a boring conversation.

But ... the "role" you were playing has allowed you to add a little spice and sex into the mix instantly...

So now you can still answer his question ... but you remained able to make the corresponding talk ... SEXY.

How to Make a Short Talk Sexy - Technique # 2:

Turn conversation into a "game" and allow mutual interaction to take on a life of its own. Have you ever had hours of fun just throwing a tennis ball against a wall and catching it when it came back to you?
Or, didn't you step on the cracks' when you were walking down a sidewalk?
Or, did you try to pass as many cars as you were driving on a highway? Or, sit at your desk and rate "how sexy" the girls in your classroom were ... while your teacher gave a devious explanation?

If you've done any of these things ...
... You have found THE GAME to make something boring fun
 We do it all the time ... because games are so much fun!

# "GETTING THE GAME"

Every cooperation you have with a gal has the potential for a game, and once you get that game, what used to be a boring, normal conversation becomes something you are a part of.

Whether as teammates or as competitors ...
You just have to find something that simplifies your interaction, that you can turn into a kind of contest and see who can beat the other.

Everyone likes to play games because the rules are simple and clear. ... And just like playing a "role,"... These games allow the occurrence of things to be much easier to say ... because the conversation comes from the game ...
Before we get into some examples of "games" you can play ... let's examine some of the reasons they are so effective at making sexy little talk ...
Why "Games" Work So Well ...
They create a sense of comfort between the two (for good)
They keep the conversation flowing smoothly ... creating the illusion of "chemistry."
They allow both of you to share information that you would not otherwise have.

They make it much easier to introduce the element of "sexuality" into the conversation.

They focus the conversation on feelings, emotions, and observations ... rather than facts. The truth is ... THE SHORT TALK MUST BE TAKEN ... there is some information that needs to be passed back and forth between you and a woman ...
... But just like sitting down to listen to a boring lecture, being stuck on the road, or taking a walk down the street ...

*SHORT TALK can BECOME FUN by finding the game ...*
What are games?
Any activity that can be used for fun ...
But to make this explanation much simpler, I will list some of the most popular games that the best Ligue Artists use regularly.

Each of these games is designed to provoke emotions in the woman you are talking to ... and create the feeling of comfort and ATTRACTION. ... Here are some of my favorites.

Just remember that just like when you use "paper," you MUST NOT explain the games. Just jump to them. Start with something fun and high-energy and slowly go deeper and more sincere.

**Game of three questions**

While talking to a girl, the game just starts ...
You: "Let's play a little game."
Her: "Okay, what kind of game?"
You: "It's very simple; we just take turns asking each other questions ... but there are rules."
Her: "Such as ...?"
You: "1) Each question must be acknowledged, 2) No question can be reproduced, and 3) you go first ..."
"So, I want to understand more about you ... What is ... your favorite ice cream? Mine is Ben and Jerry's Cookie ..."
Trade three questions back and forth. You ask, she answers. Then she asks questions, and you answer.
Start with very common or very funny things (for example, "what is your preferred ice cream?"), And be qualified to share your answer and get the game going.
The second question is a little deeper; you can talk about good childhood memories.
In the third question, go deeper; it can be about love, relationships, etc. Since it is a game, she will be speechless when you ask her, "Where was the most unusual place you had sex?"

You just give her a smile that says, "Yeah, I just asked ..."
Unless she's prudish, he's going to go the way you carved.

Can you see how simple it was to introduce sexuality into the conversation under the guise of a game?

Every time I use it, the girl asks something sexual in less than five questions.

Fascination Game / Like Game

This is another great way to share information fun and creates a playful back and forth between you ...

Fascinates me ... I like it ...

Remember, start small. Don't go straight to the deep stuff. Make her speak first and go deep little by little.

E.g., "Do you know what I like about New York? Who has the best pizza in the world. What do you like about New York?"

Then once you've warmed up ... "I love girls who have an unusual side ..."

It's about the "VIBES" that comes and goes between you and the girl. Rather than relentlessly trying to create a deep sense of comfort ... just focus on the vibe that's going on between the two of you.

Interaction should be the center of attention .... NOT the TOPIC being discussed.

I repeat: Interaction should be the center of attention ... It is NOT the TOPIC being discussed.

This is where I had completely spoiled it in the previous story. I made "healthy food" and "Gary Null" the center of attention when attention must have been the playful interaction between the two.
Now I wonder - what if the interaction with the girl "Gary Null" had been as follows instead?
Me: I like peanut butter smoothies
Her: I like Graham Cracker Nutrition Bars
Me: (giving him those five) Me too ... I also like to travel to spontaneous places and strange dark places.

Her: Oh yeah ... Well, I like to watch people walking along the boardwalk and laugh at everyone who seems strange to me.
Me: Well, I like to have sex on the beach while "strangers" walk the boardwalk.

Her: I like sex after getting back from a really hard workout at the gym ...

See how planning a game allows you to elevate the discussion to a sexual level ... in a matter of minutes?

When you put something in the meaning of a "character" or "a game," the woman's statement goes downhill, and she finds herself playing along ... BECAUSE IT'S FUN.

Remember that a woman is looking for fun. And frankly, most men are bored and incapable of entertaining

conversation (I know that because I was one of them), so
when a woman meets a guy who can create laid-back fun
... she instantly will recognize "this guy is different "and
will play your game.
Yes, she wants to play your game ...
She just has to be sure it's going to be something nice ...

# PLAYING ROLES

What is playing a role?

It is creating an imaginary setting and characters that the two of you can move out together. Let's say you're speaking to a girl, and you tell her you're going to Italy next week ... and she humorously says, "can I go ...?"

Instead of laughing at this ... you would say something like:

"Yes, I'm going to hide you in my suitcase ... When you get there, you have to be my paparazzi. I'm going to provide you a camera, and you just have to follow me around all the time, taking pictures of me ... and pointing at me like I'm someone famous. Then you can sell the images to a local tabloid, and we can use the money to take a yacht and play in Monaco. Of course, I'm going to end up losing you in a game of poker against some Iranian sheik ..."

You see how you just caught this absurd position and kept making it more absurd.

She was playful though, you probably got her to laugh ... and she predicted a future where the both of you were in Italy and Monaco. It's very manageable.

Start a story about a daydream with you and her. Let me fill in some details and together create a fun game.

And for the love of God ... don't be afraid to introduce a little sexuality into the role play ... that's what it's all about ...
So... there you have it!
Some of my preferred ways to combine fun, playfulness, and sexuality to your short talks ... and MASSIVELY increase your appeal in the eyes of the woman you are interacting with. And what's great about all the techniques mentioned is that you don't need to change what you're talking about ... just how you present the information.

Now is the time for you to put these techniques into practice and get a little RESULTS. Take my word for it ...

# START NOW!

Take action right now — don't wait. Do something with what you've learned right away, so you can start using it AUTOMATICALLY. Use these techniques every day, and soon you will realize that you will create the kind of vibe that women crave, and you can almost see that attraction shining in their eyes ...

# HOW TO FLATTER A WOMAN EFFECTIVELY

Suppose That a person admires him. Is this enough in itself for someone to like you? Probably not. If your value is too high than that of the others, they will get nervous around you, and you will perceive that both do not have good chemistry together because they do not feel very good around them when they are around you. This happens because they see you much better than they see themselves.

And this is a problem faced by many people who are perceived as "cool" or "cool." Although they look like very cool people, others feel stage fright around them.

As a consequence, many great people have trouble maintaining relationships (sex and friendships.) So your cool and cool must be balanced by allowing other people you interact with to feel good about themselves in your presence.

You are wondering, "How is this done?" You do this by freely handing out genuine compliments.

One method to do this is to make a flattering remark and then quickly ask a question below in a probing manner as if ensuring that said woman is qualified to be with you. Remember, you are a good match, so she will feel good when you impress him.

Examples-

You: "What? You have a good vibe! What do you do for fun?"

She: "Blah, blah."

You (thinking about it for a second): "That sounds like a lot of fun. I would love to hear more about that."

You: You look cool to me. What do you say you are studying? "

She: "Blah, blah."

You: "Interesting ... I have a friend who studied Bla Bla."

You see, when you say a genuine compliment, quickly follow up with a question. This also prevents the woman from denying compliance and puts her to the test.

She will be practically eating out of your hand and believing what you tell her as long as you make her feel qualified to be with you.

As an alpha male, you approve, and you don't need an approval return. So don't expect her to thank you for the compliment.

AlsoYes, women typically deny compliments or flattery while making them look less brilliant. And women may then think that you gave false praise, which is the last thing you want. So don't give him a chance to deny your praise.

I like to follow up on my compliments with a question because then that frames the interaction as that even though I found something I liked about it, my approval can still go away if I don't like your next answer. That makes me the highest value token, and it's her job to win my affections. She will be a little happier when she sees that you are interested in the answer.

Now here's something you need to know: you mustn't give false compliments because you would be trying too hard to get approved. Also, it's hard to give a fake compliment and make it sound sincere, and you don't want her to get suspicious. And this is what beats do, and alphas do not.

Another strategy I like, particularly with a new woman, is to change the subject or issue after paying the compliment quickly. "You strike me as a very interesting girl. You know what? Something happened to me on the way
..."
And this keeps me in control of the direction of the conversation and prevents her from having a chance to deny my compliment.

Another reason why I like to dish out compliments in my interactions with people that it keeps me externally focused. Because I am thinking about them, I do not care or burden myself to analyze my every move.

# JUST ONE LOOK

Learn to conquer it in 4.5 seconds; just one look is enough!

Eye contact is key when flirting is no mystery.

Although body language also sends messages, according to experts, eye contact is the most effective method to conquer. For something, they say that the eyes are windows to your heart and that your gaze is more communicative than you imagine.

80% of the information you receive enters through the eyes and is the most receptive sense. When someone is looking at you, you immediately notice, and your brain begins to take mental notes about that person depending on how they are looking at you.

For example, if your brain perceives that someone is looking at you simultaneously as many people, it stops recording information and discards it. On the other hand, if they are only looking at you, they will alert you, and you will feel the need to look at them again.

So eye contact is vital for communicating all kinds of emotions, particularly attraction signals, making it the most important resource when flirting. And there are five infallible techniques to achieve it (without looking crazy).

# MAINTAIN EYE CONTACT FOR 4.5 SECONDS

When you look at someone, it takes your brain three seconds to scan their face, so doing it for a second and a half long is a way of letting them know that they held your attention longer than anyone else. But beware! Holding it for ten seconds will be sending one of two messages: you want to have sex, or you are about to fight over something.

After all, looks are one of the best foreplay to have good sex.

Sustained eye contact for a long time produces very strong emotional reactions. Besides, it activates the nervous system, raises the pulse, and stimulates blood circulation. So as subtle as it may sound, holding your gaze for a few seconds is a clear sign of flirting.

# LOOK AT IT, LOOK AWAY, AND LOOK AT IT AGAIN!

When you are with other people, it can be more difficult to flirt.

The trick is to have eye contact with the person you are interested in, and while they are looking at you, look at the rest of the people, and then look at them again. This is the most effective way to let her know that he was the first person to attract you, and even if you have looked at the rest, he is still the one who interests you.

And if you are alone with her, you can also put it into practice!

Let her understand that you are interested in breaking eye contact by looking down and then looking up again.

On the other hand, if his gaze drifts to the side or up immediately after making eye contact and he does not look at you again, he is most likely not interested.

Follow this advice, and in 10-15 seconds, you will have your answer: either you have conquered it, or you should definitely take another look at the others - maybe there is someone else that you discarded very quickly.

# THE TRIANGLE

According to various eye movement studies, when we make eye contact with other people, our gaze tends to rest on strategic points on their faces.

When looking at a stranger or in professional situations, we usually make a triangle from one eye to the other and end in the space between the nose and the mouth.

In friendlier situations, the triangle widens, and we look down at the mouth.

On the other hand, with people who seem attractive to us, we tend to lower our gaze much lower, including our chest (yes, you know why men cannot contain themselves, it's a natural reaction!).

And the more intense the flirting gets, the quicker, more passionate, and more constant eye contact becomes, followed by long periods spent at the mouth.

# BLINK

If the movies have taught us anything, blinking is a clear form of flirting, but it works! The truth is that when you're looking at someone you like, you tend to blink more than normal.

It's been proven that the brain associates blinking with attraction, so the more you blink, the clearer it is that they like you. And the greatest thing is that it is reciprocal; when you feel that someone blinks at you more attracted you will feel towards that person.

So use it to your advantage!

Increase the frequency with which you blink, and if he unconsciously likes you, he will synchronize with you, increasing the level of attraction between the two of you. Of course, now do not shy away if he blinks a little because it does not mean that he is disinterested.

When you are completely absorbed in a conversation, busy or very entertained, you blink less so you don't miss a second.

But what then?

Use common sense, analyze his body language and the situation, and it will be clear to you if he is flirting with you back or not.

# STING HER EYE

The classic, incomparable and infallible wink or eye sting.

Accompany her with a sexy smile; it is a very effective way of letting her know that you are connected with her. And if you want to be more daring, try it with both eyes at the same time.

Before you start juggling, what we mean is blink in practically slow motion.

But considering that blinking takes milliseconds in slow motion does not mean that you close your eyes (freak). Just consciously blink once a little more slowly.

*Now, if you are ready to go out and conquer with your best weapon: your eyes.*

Everything is valid in war and love, right?

# THE SECRETS OF EYE CONTACT

Contact is very important when it comes to communication. Not only serve to modulate the conversation and convey feelings and ideas. Learning to crack their codes can give you a lot of information about others.

Eye communication is a powerful means of expression. Through looks, conscious and unconscious messages are sent that exert great influence in all kinds of encounters. They are part of that communication between the lines that mark so much mutual perception. The looks are a world to decipher that is worth taking into account.

Eye contact and its interpretation are strongly associated with the amygdala, a part of the brain related to emotions. Now, the fascinating thing about eye contact is that it is subtle and forceful language at the same time.

We are not aware of how we look, and sometimes we do not even reflect on the message we are communicating and what effects it has on interaction with others. This article's objective is precisely to elucidate some interesting points of the wonderful world of the gaze.

*"Who does not assume a look will not assume a long explanation."*

-Arabic proverb-

# EYE READING

All eyes convey some excitement, even when they are not very powerful. In the latter, the aridity of the experience or the apathy experienced is reflected. However, it is not easy to observe at a glance. The other person may be upset. Now, when we do, we discover in her the traces of her emotional world.

Scholars of body language have managed to identify several of the encrypted codes in eye contact. Here are some of the most common interpretations:

If the blinking is excessive and noticeable, you probably feel insecure and nervous. People don't believe in leaders who blink too much.
They are looking to the left means to remember something and to the right to generate thoughts or ideas. If your gaze is constantly looking in that direction, that person may be lying. With left-handed people, this goes the other way around.
When someone looks into their eyes, they do not believe what the other person is saying.
If there is a concern in keeping good communication with the other, it is usual that the eyebrows are raised during the conversation.

# SEDUCTION AND INSTINCT

Looks also perform an essential role during seduction. They are usually the inception of what later becomes a kind bond. Even if the contact is by phone, the people's eyes reflect a certain love interest. For example, it is usual that they shine more, that the pupil is more dilated, and reflect more sweetness.

# According To Body Language Experts, Interest In Another Person Is Measured In Eye Contact.

If a person stares you in the eye, lowers their gaze, and then looks back at you, they are probably interested in you.

If the person looks at you, then breaks contact and looks to the side, they are not sure if they are brought to you or not.

If she makes eye contact but then looks up, she will most likely not feel any attraction to you. When you blink more than ten times a minute, you are interested in the person in front of you. Animals are also susceptible to the gaze of humans. If they are angry, they interpret the gaze as a posture of defiance. Looking away is one way to reduce the possibility of an attack.

In conclusion, looks are a world of infinite possibilities. A way of communicating that says a lot about ourselves and others. Therefore, it is worth getting into account when communicating with other people.

# THE POWER OF THE GAZE

They say that the gaze is a door to the soul. Through it, we can know many things about the person who is looking at us. There are all kinds of looks, and these also change depending on the moment and the emotional state of the person. It is not the same to look with anger as to look with desire, passion, or indifference...

Thus, the information that a glance can convey is enormous, especially if that look is sincere. This is so because the looks are usually very expressive, although it depends on their type. Eye contact is one of the weapons of seduction, which we use in many cases to transmit things to the other person and awaken something in them.

If we learn to use the gaze well and accompany it with other aspects or actions that we will see in this article, we will be able to seduce someone effectively, or if not, to awaken their interest in us. Flirting with your eyes but is not easy, and we must take into account several aspects.

First of all, clarify that this article in no way pretends to be a manual to flirt, far from it. We will talk about the power of the look when it comes to seducing and some aspects concerning it that you can enhance to have a more marked effect on the other person.

While we talk about seducing, we also refer to awakening the interest of another person beyond a sexual or love sense ... although it is true that throughout the article, we will frequently refer to the action of flirting.

You were flirting with your eyes: how to do it effectively?

# BUT, HOW TO CONNECT WITH THE LOOK? AND
ABOVE ALL, HOW TO DO IT SUCCESSFULLY? WE ARE GOING TO ANALYZE SOME ASPECTS THAT CAN HELP US TO ACHIEVE THIS:

- Attitude

The first point that we must be clear about when connecting with the gaze is that the gaze that we project or direct to the other has to be accompanied by an attitude. This attitude must be consistent with what we are trying to convey with our eyes. Simply "looking" is not the same as looking with desire or passion, for example.

Thus, the attitude has a lot to do with the purpose of our gaze and with the emotion that we want to transmit and that we want to awaken in the other.

We must ask ourselves, what do we want to awaken in the other, exactly? Do we want to arouse interest? Desire? Curiosity? And based on this, "adjust" our gaze. For this, we can practice in the mirror.

- Time

On the other hand, the idea is that the look that we give to another person lasts only a few seconds (even thousandths of seconds). Very long glances are not effective because they can cause just the opposite effect, that the other person becomes overwhelmed or intimidated.

- Intensity

Another aspect to consider to link with the gaze is its intensity and how we modulate it. This characteristic is not easy to define since how do we measure the intensity of a gaze? This is, in a way, a matter of common sense.

We can look very intensely (fixedly, without blinking, with an accompanying facial expression) or, at the opposite extreme, look "without further ado" in passing and without being too entertained.

So the intensity of flirting with the gaze also has to do with the duration of the gaze and with the facial expression as a whole, among others. Ideally, then, it will turn out to find a middle point in this intensity; for this, we can practice in a mirror, for example.

- Body language

The look is one of the body language elements (within a non-verbal language), but more.

To link with the gaze effectively, we must also attend to other aspects of our body that accompany that gaze so that they are consistent with it (that is, the idea is that there is a certain harmony between our gaze and the rest of the body).

We must think that the look largely defines our facial expression and face since it is one of its key points. For this reason, we must look at:

- Smile

Do we want to accompany our gaze with a smile? If so, what type? A mischievous smile, perhaps? Everything is important when it comes to flirting!

- Posture

What body posture will accompany that look? Ideally, it should be a natural posture and never forced.

- Gestures

What gestures will accompany our smile? We must also keep this aspect in mind and modulate it to be consistent with our gaze and expression. Let us remember that if the different verbal language elements "agree," our message will reach more effectively and credibly.

- Hands

The position of the hands is also important, although not always excessively. It all depends on the context in which we are flirting with the other person. Thus, it is not the same to be standing as sitting, far as to close, in a cinema as in a museum, etc.

- Set your goal

But, as mentioned earlier, none of those is useful when flirting with your gaze if you don't previously set your "goal." This includes finding the time to look at that special someone, so you must get that crossing of eyes first of all.

How to interpret the reaction of the other?
Okay, okay ... we have put into practice our best look at that person who steals our sleep, but ... what happened then? What has she done? Different situations can occur. We show you some of them and how to interpret them.

- She keeps his gaze It.

Maybe that, while we are looking at her, the other person has also kept his gaze on ours. What can this mean? One possibility is that we have interested her, or at least, we have aroused some curiosity in her.

- Withdraws look

It can also occur just the opposite, and it looked to withdraw. If you do it right when eye contact occurs, this may be a sign of embarrassment or intimidation.

If you do it a little later, it may mean the same thing or simply that we have annoyed you or that you have no interest in us (although it is too early to judge). It will also depend on whether it was the first time we did it or not.

- Withdraw your gaze and fix it again

If the other person withdraws their gaze to fix it on us again, this may be an indicator of interest.

- Game of looks and smile

When it comes to flirting with the look, if the other person reacts "playing" with their eyes and accompanies everything with a smile, this seems to be a good indication that they like simply that he is interested in meeting you.

- Avoid your gaze and do not look again.

If the other person not only withdraws his gaze once we establish eye contact but also avoids your gaze and does not look at you again, this is a likely indication that he has no interest in you.

Logically, this and the previous tips should be analyzed in their global context and consider other aspects of the interaction, so they only offer guidance when interpreting the game of gazes and the other person's reaction.

# HOW TO SEDUCE SOMEONE WITH YOUR EYES

The eyes can be a powerful tool for seduction. There are various ways you can practice your eyes to show attraction and get someone interested in you. Make initial eye contact and make the most of your gaze.

- Take the initiative to make initial eye contact. This shows confidence, which many people find beautiful. People tend to be involved in those who are interested in them. Intrigue a person if you try to match their gaze from across the room. Try to make eye connections first, rather than waiting for her to notice you. Look for signs that someone is interested in you. Use this as an opportunity to make initial eye contact. The cues can be subtle, like someone glancing at you. Women can sometimes run their fingers through their hair to convey attraction.

- Start with a few brief looks. Start things off with a few glances if you are a shy person. Looking at someone twice definitely conveys an interest. Try a few short glances at someone, look away, and then see them again. This can show a potential partner that you are attracted to and that you want their attention.

- Look at someone sideways. In addition to making direct eye contact, seeing someone out of the corner of your eye can be helpful. Only glance at someone for a few minutes if they haven't had a chance to strike up a conversation yet.

Spend about 5-10 minutes looking sideways at a person you find attractive. Be cool and make it obvious. See if that person also notices you.

It can help look at someone out of the corner of your eye while laughing at something a friend says. Laughter is contagious and can be attractive to the person you are trying to seduce.

# LOOK BETTER THAN YOU EVER

The physique is important, but not as much as you think. And not how you think. Women don't rely on how you look to judge men the way we men judge how pretty our girlfriends are. Look at it this way: imagine you are on vacation and meet a chubby girl at a tropical bar who is just as hot as you. You don't have prospects for the night, so what would you rather have, have sex with this fat girl that no one will find out about, or masturbating alone in your room?

*Most guys would choose the above. Assuming it's not unpleasant - just a little overweight.*

Women act the same way. As long as they reach a particular standard — that is, you are not morbidly obese or deformed in some way — you will not be eliminated due to their ugly packaging. Appearance makes up perhaps 20% of your level of attractiveness. (level of confidence, how comfortable you are with yourself, how high your status is in society, and how you make women feel in your presence are the other factors.) If Johnny Deep — a guy who is a 10 in appearance (according to my girlfriend) —were currently a depressed "rag" who is gangly all the time and trembles at the thought of talking to the girls he just met, he would have nothing. Of success.

So, balancing it all out, looking good will certainly add a lot to your appeal. And in this chapter, you will discover the secrets to change your appearance, which will immediately double or triple the looks towards you.

# SHOES

women notice them much more than men. Many guys only have a few pairs of shoes in their closets. Have you seen how many pairs the average woman has? Girls, pay attention to what you wear. So make sure your shoes are pretty and stylish and even a bit bolder than the plain shoes the average guy would wear.
When in a shoe store, definitely ask women about shoes before you buy them! You don't want to make a costly mistake. Just say, "I need a quick female opinion. What shoes do you like, this pair or this one? "I recommend picking the two pairs that you like the best and asking for their opinion then.

Don't worry if the woman doesn't like any, and she will probably find other shoes in the store and let you know which ones she prefers. (In the meantime, you will have an opportunity to start a conversation with a girl, you naughty dog!)

At a minimum, you will need four pairs of shoes:

1) casual chestnut.
2) casual black.
3) elegant/formal chestnut.4) elegant/formal black.

For formal shoes, I get the type of shoes that need to be polished. You will pay a lot for such shoes like that (my elegant black shoes cost $ 150), but they last for years so that they will be worth the expense. When they're polished up well, I get a lot of compliments. (I've noticed that women like polished shoes.)

# HAIR

If you're like most men, your hair doesn't look very good right now. Maybe you've had the same hairstyle for years or are trying to do the same thing with their hair that their friends do with theirs, even though their hair is different. It is time for a change. Check out what Hollywood actors and rock stars are up to now, find a hairstyle you like, and style yours later. Experiment. As I write this guide, the "sex hairstyle" (messy hair that makes him look like you've just been in bed with a woman) hits hard. Consider going to an expensive stylist and giving him carte blanche to style your head shape well.

If you want to look sexy (and you're not homophobic), I highly recommend going to a gay hairdresser, as these guys have an almost uncanny sense of what looks good for women. And honestly, if your hairline has gotten to the point where it's too noticeable, then shave your head. A significant percentage of women consider a shaved head attractive because baldness exudes masculinity and vigor. If you are an older man, having your head shaved will make you look a few years younger. Combing your hair is fooling no one, and few women find horseshoe-shaped hair sexually attractive.

# THE SKIN

One of the simplest (and free) things you can do to improve sex appeal with women is to get a tan. You don't want to go overboard with this as there is a risk of skin cancer, but sunlight is also necessary to get the proper vitamin D dose, which helps your body produce testosterone. (Also, a lack of sunlight has been associated with a depressed mood.) If anything, though, get a good tan, and women will think you are sexy. You can kill two birds with one stone by exercising outside.

# THE SHAVE

Beards or mustaches are generally out of style these days unless you find a certain look that goes with their features or if you have any deficiencies that you need to hide. For example, a goatee or beard can work wonders to disguise a weak chin or acne-scarred cheeks. Consider shaving your testicles and the pubic hair that grows around the base of your penis. If you do, your penis will appear cleaner and more attractive to women. They will give you blowjobs more often. Just as we prefer women to shave their vulvas (since all that hair gets in the way), women also prefer you to shave. And as a bonus, your penis will appear to be longer without all that hair around it. Don't get picky. Shaving your scrotum is much easier than you think. Try it with shaving cream and a razor. Shaved hair will come out smoothly. Shaving your armpits can reduce the number of bacteria that grow under your arms, reducing body odors.

Also, make sure you do not have hair from your nose or hair sticking out of your ear. Many women lose any stimulus when encountering this. You can find an electric nasal hair clipper at your local grocery store for less than $ 20.

Many men shave their breasts these days, as more women seem to prefer shaved breasts to hairy breasts.

However, that is an individual option. If you don't mind this, I suggest you try to see the reactions you get when you shave your chest and wear a shirt that exposes it. If you are tempted to shave your arms or legs, fight the urge and don't. The bottom line is that the vast majority of men who do this are a) professional bodybuilders or b) gay.

# STRETCH

For casual occasions, wear shirts that fit well, not shirts that appear too baggy. This can be harsh, as most clothes that you like will not fit. Just hope that about 10% of the clothes you try on in a store will be favorable to you. I can't stress enough the importance of not wearing baggy clothes and tents in vogue in ghetto high schools or among youngsters. Such clothes will not hide your tummy.

The best way to hide that rim is to wear shirts that draw attention to the chest, such as shirts with a horizontal stripe at the nipples. If you are fat, it goes without saying that you should also go to the gym (weight lifting and cardiovascular work) and eat correctly to lose weight. This also helps you with your testosterone levels. Carrying excess body fat (about 20% or more of your ideal body weight) can cause your body to have elevated estrogen levels. (Have you noticed that really fat guys sometimes have "woman's boobs"? Now you know why.)

Wear clothing that makes you appear as close to the ideal body as possible for a tall man with broad shoulders that descends to a narrow, slim waist. This is the look that women find attractive! Avoid clothing that makes you look different from this ideal body type. For example, fat guys should avoid shirts with horizontal stripes around the waist. If you are tall and slim, try a long-sleeved unbuttoned jacket or shirt over a tight T-shirt. The horizontal stripes are good; vertical stripes are bad. Common types should avoid horizontal stripes, however, as they make them look too wide. Instead, they should think about tight clothing options: tight shirts and pants. Stay away from something too common like skinny stripes or the ubiquitous polo shirts frat boys wear. No, girls won't think you're original by flipping the necklace since too many guys do that.

Company or sports logos on your shirts? That makes him look like he's trying hard to fit in with the group. That's fine if you want to be a funky guy rather than a loser, but it's more attractive to girls if you stand out from the pack of guys who roam around like signs. By dressing casually, you want to give the impression that you just dressed after having good sex with a woman. So don't wrap your shirt completely unless you're wearing a suit. And leave the top two buttons unbuttoned.

Avoid weird designs or whatever makes you look like you're trying too hard to look cool. Consider wearing a suit and tie sometimes, especially when you're in situations where other guys dress like lotus, like in college. Have you ever noticed how women go out of their way just to flatter dudes in suits and ties? Suit and tie are important executive clothing. And they communicate status and ambition, and there is no counterpart for wearing them. Of course, you have to make sure you are an alpha inside, or you will be taken by a nerd trying to make a good impression.

When wearing a suit, wear a cotton shirt (plain, no stripes or anything), cufflinks, a dark jacket and pants, and a black leather strap, shoes well polished. Wear a nice silk tie, which can even have a bold design. Notice the type of compliments you get from people. Nothing expresses authority better than a dark suit. Vintage clothing is in, as long as it is not too flashy. Jeans are also good. Try to get a pair of expensive jeans. Go for a slim size because you want to make your legs look slim.

# COMBINING

I'm continually in awe of how many guys I see make obvious mistakes like wearing brown belts with black shoes, so please pay attention to how the colors of their outfits go together.

You need to match all your clothes. You can do this two ways:

1) Through similar colors.
2) Through significantly contrasting colors.

Colors tend to affect people's spirits and energy levels, so think about what you want to provoke when you dress up and then combine the parts of your outfit accordingly.
There are two main sections — hot and cold. Warm colors include yellow, orange, and red. Cool colors include purple, blue, and green. If you want to wear similar colors, wear different shades of one color, such as light jeans and a darker blue shirt. You can also try colors that are closely close — red and purple. For example, both colors are close to each other on the color wheel. Also, dress in opposite ends of the color wheel — dark blue pants with a light brown shirt. Neutral colors — black and white — go with almost everything. Also, consider using colors primarily white or black — like beige, white tinged

with brown or gray, a combination of black and white. But not beige with gray.

The color of your accessories (belt, watch, etc.) should match your shoes as much as possible. Pants should never contrast too much with your shoes, although your shirt can. Another rule for clothing that should be obvious, but often is not, is that clothing should be clean. Girls more easily detect stains and unwashed clothes.
How do you know if your clothes need to be washed?

**1)**On shirts and pants, look for stains. If you see stains, wash them by rinsing the stain under a tap and rubbing it off with the stain remover. Then put the garment in the washing machine.

**2)** Socks and clothes should only be worn once before being washed.

**3)** Jeans need to be washed when they stretch, even if they are not stained.

**4)**Nothing should smell. If it smells, put it in the laundry basket.

Ironing is not as necessary as it used to be, except in extreme cases. However, some things should always be ironed, like Oxford shirts (the long-sleeved cotton shirts you wear a suit with). When dressing in a suit, make sure your shirt is slightly starchy, or else you won't look good. You don't have to do the ironing ... just take your things to dry cleaning and let them do it.

Another thing that women appreciate is attractive underwear, as they wear flashy panties. So get something with something written on the garment or a drawing. One night, with my current girlfriend, she was fascinated by my SpongeBob shorts. Short, dark-colored garments are also an excellent option.

# ACCESSORIES

Most guys don't pick their accessories well, so this is a good area for distinguishing yourself from the rest. The main thing is that these are subtle but intriguing. Avoid overdoing it or trying too hard. Find interesting things that fit your personality. A $ 30 watch with a wide leather strap displaying a unique design will send you more compliments from women than a multithousand silver watch as the former displays much more originality.

A pretty $ 15 faux silver ring with an eye-catching pattern will turn the heads of women 100 times more than a $ 500 college class ring. There is wide latitude for accessories, as long as they make you stand out from the other types. Try to avoid things that tons of other guys already have, like white snail necklaces and bracelet tattoos. Be unique.

# YOUR STYLE

There are two types of subjects — those who have sex and those who do not. To have sex, figure out which demographic of people you belong to (e.g., high school guys, corporate executives, ghetto boys, college kids), observe the alpha males' dress in that group, and dress similarly. In particular, just try to be a little "cooler" than everyone else when it comes to shoes, accessories like your belt and watches, and the way your clothes fit. (Make sure you resemble the ideal of the male body described above.)

Don't look much "cooler" than everyone else, or you might seem out of place and weird, or even gay. Just be a little bit better dressed than the best-dressed guy around. Take a look around, and it will be obvious how you should dress and what you should avoid. For example, T-shirts with sports logos, beer bottles, or phrases that you wouldn't say in a decent company are not attractive to women and are typically only worn by guys who will be out of luck that night.

Watch the latest blockbuster movies with popular actors for fashion advice. (The movie "The Big Scam 2" has some good examples of it currently being hit.) Also, check out TV and magazine ads targeting 18- to 35-year-old demographics. I'm not talking about ads for clothing per se (as these tend to go for very expensive clothes), but ads for things like cell phones and airlines. The models in these advertisements generally dress subtly well so that they attract a larger audience.

When you're shopping for clothes, listen to the opinions of the women in the store.
Simultaneously, create your unique style and avoid styles that are too ordinary and too flat. I like to shop around and dress in brighter, tighter 80's clothes. This is because it fits my personality. So go for something unique and trendy that is appropriate for you, but don't get too complicated by how it looks either. Because while looking for good bits of help, it's not your looks that drive you to bed; it's your alpha male behaviors and thought patterns.

Women are not just after a handsome man. They also ask for a man with high social status and excitement, passion, and romance. They want a man who will give them a good time and make them feel good. Along with style issues, it is also important to develop a strong male body. That means going to a gym and having a good diet.
Going to a gym will not only make you look healthier, but it will also make you feel more energetic and attractive to women because you will have much more confidence.

The most important thing about how you look is that it should be consistent and congruent with who you are. Your clothes create perceptions of you in women. So if you can't support such created perceptions, they will lose interest.
If her clothing expresses "excitement" in the way Lamborghini styling does, then women will be disappointed if the engine inside is anything conventional like that of an SUV.

# YOUR BODY

Women could guess my age before I started practicing six years ago. Sometimes they thought I was older! So about six months after I started working out at the gym, the women I knew were shocked at my age — they thought I was younger.

A few months ago, a very pretty 26-year-old woman who took me into her home swore she couldn't be over 28. (I'm 39 years old.) She genuinely didn't believe me when I told her how old I was. He used to be fat and lazy; I am now lean and muscular. On a scale of 1 to 10, my appearance would round up a 4. Whenever I put my picture on sites like hotornot.com, I generally rated around 4 to 5. Today I am rated 8 to 8.5, and for the compliments that I get from women, I would say my rating on hot or not is pretty accurate.

You can't do anything about their genetic heritage (yet). However, your fitness level is totally within your control, and it's a significant part of what makes you look good to a woman. This is good news, don't you think? Being in shape will make you look good in many ways. Your stomach will flatten out, and you will notice more defined abs. With muscles growing throughout your body, your facial muscles will also grow, making your skin firmer and less wrinkled.

# A BASIC GUIDE TO WORK THE BODY

The training I'm going to give you focuses on heavy compound exercises that work many muscles simultaneously and include isolation exercises that work many muscles that compound exercises miss. Compound exercises will be the core of your training. Away from those many guys in the gym — the ones who only work before spring break and aren't serious about it — who mostly do push-ups and bench presses ignoring their legs and back.

This leads to poor posture, and no matter how big your upper body is, skinny chicken legs don't look good. Women look at and admire men's legs. Compound exercises dump tons of testosterone into your body. Besides building muscle, having elevated natural testosterone levels are associated with dominance and power traits — two sexual traits deeply attracted to women. Do this in a typical week:

**Monday-**

- Three sets of squats. Do 20 reps, 15 reps, and then 12 reps.

(Your leg and abdominal muscles are primarily made up of slow-stretch muscle fibers that respond better to higher reps than your upper torso and back.)

- Three sets of stiff leg raises. Do 20 reps, 15 reps, and 12 reps.
- Two sets of twins raise. Do 20 reps, 15 reps, and 12 reps.
- Two sets of arm push-ups. Do 12 reps and ten reps.

(For each exercise, use a weight such that the last 3 to 5 reps are extremely difficult)

**Tuesday-**

- Rest or cardiovascular work.

**Wednesday-**

- Two sets of forwarding bent dips. Do 12 reps and ten reps.
- Two series of the press with weight to the slope. Do 12 reps and ten reps.
- Two sets of lateral raises. Do 12 reps and ten reps.
- Two sets of overhead dumbbell presses. Do 12 reps and ten reps.
- Two sets of squats with weight. Do 20 reps and 15 reps.

**Thursday-**

- Rest or cardiovascular work.

**Friday-**

- Three series of deadlifts. Do 12 reps, ten reps, and eight reps.

- Two sets of weighted chin suspension. Do 12 reps and ten reps.
- Two sets of push-ups with weights. Do 12 reps and ten reps.
- Two sets of stringing weights. Do 12 reps and ten reps.
- Two series of bends and side raises. Do 12 reps and ten reps.

Do a warm-up or before entering the main sets, using roughly 50% and 75% of your working weights. For example, if you squat 200 pounds during your main sets, you would warm up by doing eight reps of 100 pounds, then four reps of 150 pounds. You should feel the warm-up to enter your work sets. If not, then you should do 2-3 more reps with a weight closer to work. In the example, you would do three reps with 175 pounds. It is important that you feel that your strength is failing in the series. When I tell you to do sets of 20, 15, and 12, I mean do the maximum weight to support that particular number of reps.

Limit your workouts to 50 minutes. Studies have shown that after that, your muscles start to break down too quickly.

Give yourself two to three minutes between sets to recover, but remember that you want to complete all of your exercises within the 50-minute limit. Immediately after your workout, eat a mixture of protein and carbohydrates. This stops the formation of lactic acid generated by lifting weights and shifts your body towards building muscle mass.

The training I have outlined is geared towards muscle growth. If you want to emphasize strength, do half the reps. On Tuesday, Thursday, and Saturday, you should do cardiovascular work if you need to lose body fat. I recommend doing high-intensity interval training. High-intensity interval training (HIIT) is short but intense, and studies have shown it to be more effective than moderate-intensity training. Moderate training consists of activities like jogging for half an hour, etc.

HIIT lasts for 10 minutes, but it has you alternate between sprinting for one minute and jogging slowly for another minute, alternating back and forth until the 10 minutes are up. Although HIIT is much shorter than moderateintensity cardio, you are going to feel it. Finally, watch your diet. A popular saying among serious bodybuilders says, "Muscle is built in the kitchen, not the gym." To build muscle, your body needs about one gram of protein per pound of weight each day. Well, the sources are meat, chicken, nuts, tuna, and whey protein powder.

Eat smaller portions frequently rather than three large meals a day. This ensures that your body has enough protein for protein synthesis within your muscles. Eat clean, healthy calories. Avoid fats. (Look for "partially hydrogenated" oils and labels with reducing ingredients.) Avoid junk food like soda, fried foods, and white loaves of bread. Carbides are not bad by themselves; what you need is the right, complex carbohydrates, like those found in oatmeal, whole wheat bread, fresh legumes, and fruit. Avoid starches. Finally, be sure to drink plenty of fluids, as your muscles are mostly water.

# YOUR POWERS AFFECT YOUR CONDUCT.

This is the biggest reason why people who attribute things internally are more successful. Self-made millionaires tend to be people who trusted themselves and did their part to improve the situation. If you think you are attracted to women, you will find yourself displaying attractive behaviors naturally. Let's say you chat with a woman at a laundromat. You feel completely outgoing and have a great conversation with her.

After you both finish folding your clothes, you go out with her for something to eat. After a couple of hours of conversation, they head to a bar for a drink. Then they go to her house to finish everything in the bedroom. She found you attractive for many reasons, but most of all, it was his high confidence level.

So, where does your confidence come from? Does it come from having previously had sex with other women? In that case, that would be an external attribution. The problem with external attributions is that they make you vulnerable to a system of rewards and punishments. As long as you get their prize (i.e., sex with women), their confidence stays high, and you remain motivated to work out in the gym and wear good clothes.

If you have a string of failures with women, however, your confidence will plummet. So you leave the gym and wear whatever it is. So it's better to be safe because "that's the kind of guy I am" rather than whatever cause happens in the external world.

If you are confident because of your internal attributions, then you will stay that way no matter how many women don't have the good taste to choose it. (Did you notice how I didn't say, "It doesn't matter how many women reject you"? Think positively!)
By the way, there was a time when I was so terrified of talking to women that my vision would blur, my face would turn red, and I would stutter like an idiot. It was all caused by worrying about what those women thought.

*The permanent solution to this is to stop thinking that women are important.* Yes, you read that right. Thinking that women are important only gets in the way when it comes to the love game. Instead, see them as a source of excitement, arousal, and sex ... no more, no less. Don't see every woman as a potential girlfriend because that causes you to act too hard to win her approval.

# SIMPLE ALPHA MALE EXERCISE

If you find yourself with an external control site, you can help yourself get out and grow outside of it by creating a list of targets you criticize so that your life is not what it is. Go ahead and make your list right now.

Did you make your list? Very good. Some things you could have written down are:

**1)** Other people, like his parents, who did a bad job raising him or his boss who is keeping him right now. The people at your high school made fun of you and made you feel bad. These people taught him to be irrationally afraid of strangers, which is why today he is shy.

**2)** The circumstances. You were born into poverty, your uncle beat you up, you went to a bad public school, and you missed many educational opportunities that other people got.

**3)** Your genes / God. Your face is asymmetrical. You are short, etc.

I am not trying to simplify your problems at all. The key is that very often in life. We become immobilized due to circumstances that are beyond our control. Then we cannot effect a change.

We can't change how our parents raised us, so being so upset about it today is a waste of time. No matter how upset you get, you can't change what happened.
Looking at your blame list, can you see any real reason you must be so pessimistic that you do nothing to improve your life because of the people on the list?
Why do you give them that power?

Study after study has shown that firmly believing that we are in control of our situation will significantly impact our actions. The more we believe that we are not in control of our situations, the more likely we will give up.

As you move toward having an inner psychological site of control, you will become a more positive thinker. You have the power to take action to improve the things you are currently weak at. If you're ugly by example, then hit the gym, improve your diet, and work on your clothing and conditioning. You will also take responsibility for motivating yourself. You will find that as you are more determined to improve and persevere in pursuing the things you want (such as sex), you will increase your chances of getting them.

# YOUR THOUGHTS

You are constantly thinking. Most of your feelings come from thoughts. The good news is that, as thinking beings, we can choose our thoughts and thus our feelings.
We can choose to think (and feel) positively or negatively. The bad news is that it is often easier to think negatively, so we have to be positive. For example, suppose you attend a quick dating event where each woman marks "No" in the box representing your name to indicate that they do not want to see you again.

A negative view of this would be to think that you are scum, so of course, women would not want to talk to you. And what about all the other guys who were way more flashy than you? Maybe it would have been a better night if you had stayed home and played Halo 2. A positive view would be to realize that, with each girl, you wrinkled your forehead and leaned too far toward her, indicating that you were nervous and trying too hard to get her approval. Fix those two major body language mistakes, and you'll convey a better impression of yourself next time.

What you think about often becomes a part of your life. If you worry, then you will find things to worry about. If you are optimistic, then you attract good people and things. So if you want to be a successful man, you need to have positive thoughts. Remembering the past creates many negative thoughts. You have certainly erred before; it happens to all of us. The key is to forget the past.

I want to make you recognize this: the past doesn't exist anymore, except in your mind. Bury your past mistakes and don't think about them after you've learned lessons from them. Try to eliminate negative thoughts. Identify the origins of negativity in your life and do not allow them to influence you. I find negativity in certain individuals, songs, and television shows like the news. (Don't feel like you have to be a news junkie. If the world is ending, someone will let you know!)

# DEVELOP POSITIVE THINKING

Everything is in your mind. That, and your attitude. *"Why would a girl be attracted to me?"* you think. "I'm too short." You go to class and sit in your usual place. The girl sitting across from you notices you and then suddenly turns around and says, "Can you lend me a sheet?"

"Sure," you say, handing him the sheet. You don't say anything else to him for the rest of the class. That night, you remember that girl, dreaming about her while alone in bed, thinking you are a loser. What you didn't realize was that this girl was going the extra mile to talk to you. He didn't need a blade ... he could have asked another girl for it and not have to worry about the malefemale play. But she used it as an excuse to talk to you because she was interested in you. She thinks she sent you an obvious signal. But you didn't realize.

For something to happen to you, you have to believe in it first. In our example, if you had believed that you are attractive, then you would be receptive to the girls that appear in your life. But if you don't think it's a possibility, then you are psychologically blocked, even when it's obvious, like the girl who asked you for the folio.

Good things happen to you. That way, you will take advantage of the opportunities. Identify negative thoughts when they arise and let them go. As you eliminate negative thoughts, let positive thoughts flow. Choose to be confident and happy on the inside, no matter what happens on the outside. Feel comfortable with yourself and realize that you will be happy no matter what happens. Your confidence comes from yourself, and you will improve every day because that is fundamentally who you are.

Here are a few ways to develop positive thinking:

1) **Constantly imagine yourself as the person you want to be**. Imagine how you would behave and what kind of happiness you would reap in your life if you were that ideal person. Visualize the amount of money you would earn, the house you would live in, and the physique you would have. Avoid negative influences in your life, such as friends who make pessimistic comments.

2) **As you look back, think only about your successes**. Realize that any failure you have is only temporary and more the result of bad luck than any inherent problems with you.

3) **assume success**(but don't link to it). See yourself as relaxed and count on that because you are the lover of

every woman's dreams; of course, you will eventually have the success you want. Smile while having fun what makes you feel like a man who is attractive to women.

4) **Start to identify the thoughts you have**. Recognize that your judgments are under your control, so you can visualize everything you want. Because your reality is what you believe in, use your visualizations to encourage rather than discourage you. As Albert Einstein said, "your imagination is the preview of the attractions of life that are to come."

5) **Make affirmations**, which I will explain below.

# EASY ALPHA MALE EXERCISES

**1)** Identify the beliefs that are good for you.

**2)** Reinforce them by amplifying what is good for you

**3)**Identify their bad beliefs. And eliminate them.

OK, this won't happen instantly unless you fully open your mind to this and make a full effort to do these three exercises. Even if you are skeptical, if you work slowly but surely, this will pass. Take baby steps to observe your behaviors and thoughts, and isolate those thought patterns that are good and those that you want to change.
And do yourself a favor and save all your tests for later, when you're home alone, not when you're with a woman. When with a woman, stay outwardly focused and only think about the conversation at hand. This will cause you to feel relaxed and, therefore, more attractive because you are projecting confidence, which increases your likelihood of sleeping with her.

# DROWNING YOUR FEARS ABOUT REJECTION

Picture this: you are about to try to talk to a beautiful/sexy girl. You see them standing there in the magazine section of the supermarket, entertaining themselves with Cosmopolitan magazine. Her blonde hair is silky and soft. His skin is clear and radiant. His waist is slim. And wow, look at the delicious shape of those tits! You feel the tension.

Excuses explode in your head: "I'm too tired;" I'm not well dressed; "I don't know what to say to him; "I don't carry condoms. "
That negative monologue you have in your head makes you decide not to approach. Now, your chances of having sex with her are zero. You get your groceries, you go home, and you sleep alone that night. You just shot yourself; the girl did nothing.

You didn't hesitate because you were very tired or badly dressed, or the words didn't come to you (and you can always buy condoms on the way to a sexual encounter). Your real problem was fear. You didn't approach because you were afraid of rejection. "I wish I could hurry up and get over this anxiety of chatting with women ... I don't know," you say to yourself. "Once I get over it, then I will approach them eagerly / enthusiastically / smoothly."

The problem with this kind of thinking is that it sets you up for failure. The truth is that we always feel scared when we enter a new, unfamiliar situation. It is a psychological reality of human beings. The only way to free yourself from fear is to do what you need to do - for example, approach a woman despite the fear. You have to make a great effort. If you've ever done it in sports, it just is. I was so afraid to communicate with girls that my vision blurred. I continued to make these excuses that I would only approach women when my fears are gone. I kept waiting and waiting.

My fears never went away. I was immobilized, unable to figure out why I was so scared of talking to women, and I spent many days and nights refusing to do so until I could feel good instead of scared. The truth is, virtually all men have anxiety about talking to women because, let's face it, rejection sucks. We all have an internal sense of ego (e.g., self-esteem), which we wish to maintain at a high level. Ideally, your self-worth will come from within yourself, and you won't have to depend on others to have it.

When this happens, it will become irrelevant what any woman thinks of you. If he likes you, great; if not, then what does it matter? You can't control what she thinks. Don't let a woman's opinion matter too much to you. We all feel fear in an unfamiliar situation. It is normal and natural. Fear only goes away when the situation becomes familiar. If you don't make a great effort to overcome fear, you will be extremely vulnerable and paranoid. Surely, you can withdraw and stay away, and then you will never be rejected. But then you'll be lonely; you'll always be a sad loser who never slept with a girl. Here's the underlying reason: we all have an imaginary partner who will be with you your whole life. Its name is fear. If you allow this partner to control your life, he will put you in a straitjacket.

But fear can also be your faithful companion. When you jump on the exciting spinning slide of life, engaging in a myriad of challenging tasks/adventures, fear will be with you. He won't get in your way, but he will always be there as long as / as long as you're doing new things. When you feel scared, it is a sign that you are doing something new and exciting.

# HOW TO ELIMINATE YOUR FEARS

To eliminate your fears about chatting with women, you need to do three things.

**1.      Don't have expectations / Don't expect anything**. Be friendly for the sake of being social. Nothing more.

**2.      Talk to the women**. Remember that the only way to overcome your fear is by doing what you are afraid of. The more you do it, the more easily you will get there because your attitude about any kind of negative experiences like rejection will turn to something like, "I've been there, I've done that, it's not a big deal."

**3.      Identify the thoughts that make you nervous**. Then delete them. Because fear is normal, most guys feel anxious when talking to girls, especially if they are not used to it. That is why it is not about not being afraid, but that you simply go straight to what you are going to. So what sets guys like you apart from the rest is the way they handle fear.

Most of the men are paralyzed by fear. And they were necessarily concerning girls, but also in other aspects such as their career. This is why many types do not achieve the success they want.

The reason most men never confront they fear that they fail to discover where they came from. The fear comes from within you. The problem is with you, not with the woman who rejects you. So the next time you talk to women, just treat them without any expectations. Don't set goals. As I mentioned previously, I used to be an introvert. To overcome my shame, I would force myself to converse with everyone, no matter who it was.

He spoke with pretty girls, with ugly girls, with fat girls, with older people, guys, children, families walking with their dogs. It didn't matter who they were. He talked to them about neutral issues, nothing to do with raising women. The result of all this was that I became an excellent conversationalist. I never felt fear again because I could continue doing what scared me until the time came that it no longer bothered me.

Then I made a mistake. I said to myself: "Now that I am a good conversationalist and have become an easygoing person, why do I have to waste time in conversations other than with beautiful girls." After all, as an alpha male, I thought, "He was a man of high value, and I would dedicate my time only to beautiful women.

So I limited the circle of people I would talk to. And my anxiety about speaking to casual women swept me away. It was as if I had never spoken to strangers in my life. At that moment, I realized that this was. I had a dependent attitude because I had thoughts about having sex with women before I opened my mouth and said "hello," which was devastating and frustrating for my purposes.

This is the point. Here's something I want you to try. No matter where you go, talk to two people (or groups of people) only for practice. Take it very seriously. Don't try to pick up girls through these conversations. Precisely because it is to practice, do not limit yourself to talking to the best women. You are looking for simple conversations. I have found that older people (men and women over 40) and fat people are easy to start conversations with. Perhaps because that demographic tends to be lonely.

If it helps, set a time limit for your interaction practices, such as talking to one person for 30 seconds and then end the conversation (you can say something like: "OK, I'll meet a friend. It was a pleasure chatting with you And then as if it didn't matter at all).

Once you have done your internship, you will feel comfortable, and it will be easier for you to converse with the good girls. Even when and even if you feel aroused, do not think or act in a way related to sex.

For example, if a girl walks in front of you, just say something spontaneous like, "Hey, I need a female opinion on something." Then ask a question that you want their opinion on. As you gain practice, you can apply another one of my tricks to say something funny before starting a conversation with a stranger. Tell yourself a joke and then laugh. That will put you in a good mood when you talk to someone else.

Ultimately, you will get to a position where you have spoken out and gotten so many negative responses from women that it won't affect you even one bit. You will have an attitude like, "Oh, how original. I've had hundreds of women give me the same cruel response."

In the movie "Fight Club" Tyler Durden presented the following phrase: "Let things go as they should go." Stop trying to control your attitude with girls. If you don't have an attitude in mind, it won't be relevant if the girl acts like, "Now I turn my head and I remember the rejections I've received, and I laugh. I have spoken to so many women that rejections bore me, but they entertain me because of my sincerity.

To understand this more psychologically, we will say that "There is no such thing as a" State of nervousness "as something genetic. There is no such thing as "butterflies in the belly" of the "nervous virus" invading your body. All those nervous feelings come from within you. You have a series of mental processes flowing through you, and in the end, you are inclined to feel the emotion you decide.

Recently, I led a boy named James, who told me, "I would reject myself if I were a girl. So with thoughts like that, you don't have to be a witch to know why you don't succeed with women. He has a failure-oriented attitude.

We then work on the following:
1. James visualized a girl rejecting him.
2. James felt the tension in his body that was previously relaxed.
3. James evaluated every moment of the entire process, preventing him fromhaving a fluid conversation.

Perhaps it seems very familiar to you to feel nervous about a woman who is close to you? Do not be sad. Thousands of guys - even those who consider themselves "Women Charmers" - have felt it at some point. You will be there just like them.
What to do to manage nervousness: Identify your negative thoughts and then change them. Instead of thinking, "There is my God, this girl will reject me because I will not be able to speak well ... Think: How wonderful it will be to talk with this girl I just saw in the store because,

even if she rejects me, I always have the will and the conviction that every day I am one step closer to the woman of my dreams. When you are nervous, notice the parts of your body that become tense and relax your muscles in those places.

When I get nervous, I feel the tension in my face and my jaws. So I try to relax my facial muscles by mentally telling myself to relax instead of being nervous. In conclusion, there are many ways to reduce anxiety with a visualization exercise. Before you open your mouth and say something to a woman, visualize the situation as if it is happening, and then she rejects you.

Look at it this way. If you're not feeling relaxed and sexual, how do you expect the woman to cooperate? As an Alpha Male, you are obliged to lead, which means that you must feel relaxed and sexual for the girl to react favorably. That way, you'll be happy because. At least you went for it, like an alpha man who goes through life without apologizing for his wishes.

Each rejection means that you are one step closer to success. Each rejection makes your ability to converse that much better since you have completely desensitized yourself to the process. Focus on how you will feel later, and speak to the woman as if she has already rejected you (and you are happy about it) instead of making yourself nervous before you even open your mouth.

# HOW TO SUCCESSFULLY SEDUCE A WOMAN FROM ZERO

At the very smallest, you should be able to have a basic conversation with a woman. Therefore, you should make it a rule of thumb; you will have at least one long and meaningful conversation a day with a woman. It could be your sister, a platonic friend, a co-worker, or anyone. The main objective is to get used to talking to women and do it easily and naturally. By the way, when you talk to them, don't try hard to make them feel good about you. Just have a normal conversation where you can be yourself.

To get used to talking to new women, do the same; from now on, you will enter a conversation with at least four attractive women a week for a few weeks. This can be easier than it sounds if you make sure you have something to talk about beyond "Hi, where are you from?"

I said to a woman, "Hi, I need a quick feminine opinion. I'm buying my sister (mother, whoever) a perfume. What do you prefer, Fragrance X or Fragrance Y? "Unconvincing, I know, but at least this will get you in conversation with a woman you don't know. Practice your openers tackling for success; now I'm going to focus as I explain how to talk to women.

# THE APPROACH AND HOW TO DO IT

To do the boarding, you need to be in the right emotional state. You need to feel a strong sex drive and relaxed confidence. If you are nervous and fearful and thinking hard about things to say, the woman will not find you attractive and even a little creepy. I know, in an ideal world, women should be flattered that guys have a hard time talking to them about what to say to them. Perhaps, as a man who wants to sleep with her, we must adjust to reality. You must be confident, warm, and relaxed - not panic and asexual.

Remember, all girls want sex. Some have psychological blocks like frigidity, but most will have sex with you if you are an alpha man, create the right conditions for sex to occur, and lead the interaction towards having sex. Where a lot of men screw it up with women is by using an approach phrase. The problem with opening openers is that they reveal to the woman immediately before you've even had a chance to speak that you are attracted to her.

And unless you have something that makes you look handsome, you don't want her to decide whether or not she's attracted to you instantly. Instead, it is better to come under their radar. Show your alpha man personality, and then you can assume there is attraction. (I talk more about what it means to assume attraction below) Not only do you want to be under their radar, but you also want to grab their attention at the same time. Get her interested by talking to you.

Lastly, you want to have a neutral conversation with her at first. You know how defensive you get whenever you're out there walking, and some homeless man comes up to you asking, "Hi, how are you?" You get defensive when this happens because you know the bum wants your money. He is seeking trust with you too soon... since he doesn't know you, he has no reason to want to connect with you.

Well, it's the same kind of reaction with women. When you approach a girl trying to seek confidence immediately, her defensive shield blocks you. On the contrary, when you have a normal, neutral conversation with the girl, she doesn't have those initial shields. And once you have that initial shield with a woman, as long as you have a normal conversation and take on the report (more on this later too), then you will find yourself having breakfast in your underwear with her the next morning, as long as you are persistent and sexual.

For that reason, there is what I like to call "Nine Hypnotic Words." These cover all of the bases I've listed before (putting yourself under a girl's radar, getting her attention, getting her interest in the initial conversation, and being completely neutral). The number one thing you have to say to a girl you randomly meet is, "Hi, I need a swift female viewpoint on something."

If you get their opinion on this, you can be extremely flexible, but make sure this topic is interesting for women examples:

- Did you read something in the last issue of the Cosmopolitan
- What do you think of this shirt?
- I am thinking of buying this painting. What do you think of it?
- When a woman asks me if her clothes make her look fat, what should I say?
- Tell him about a date situation that a friend (man) of yours had in front of a girl.
- My friend only studied with this girl all day.

- She tore a sheet out of her book and threw him like a paper airplane. She laughed, and he smiled. Then he wanted to do the same, but she suddenly got serious and said, 'No' don't do this; he told me he looked like an idiot. And he wondered, what should he have done?

- Ask. "If your lover plays video games all day. How would you feel about this? Then go inside the story about how your friend's girlfriend left him because he played every day.

- Start a discussion about what is going on back then. For example, if you are going to a dog rescue event, talk about the animals up! Adoption • Nice weather today (especially if it isn't). You have to try this kind of peppermint (Say this at the grocery store). What do you think?

- You can converse with a girl about virtually anything, as long as you are neutral.

But be sure that it is a topic that interests you as well. That way, you seem genuine and not like you are trying to win her over. Also, never recite the memorized material! I only use the above list as topics of conversation, not as scripts. Trust me, and this took me a while to learn; if you look like a stage agent reciting lines, you will crash and burn.

Another key point (which took me a long time to finally figure out) When you start the conversation, make sure you don't seem too polished or like it's too easy to talk to her. If not, she will say something like, "Are you a seller of something?" or "I had to meet him sooner" Instead of just being normal (laid back and carefree)!

Your main thing to talk about can be as simple as your immediate environment. If you are in a movie theater, ask her if she has ever seen a particular movie and what she thinks of it. Tell you a story about something interesting that happened to you before the movie. One of my stories from the movies I told a girl I conquered in a movie theater and eventual romance:

I took one of my previous girlfriends to see a movie, and it was just the two of us and these eight teenagers. They were all loud and annoying, but before the movie started. My girlfriend got upset and said, "You can shut up. I want to see the movie, thank you!" They all gave me a bad look because, as men, you cannot fight with women, but you can fight with other men.

After a while, I went to the bathroom, and there they were all. I felt like they were all about to hit me. But then they told me, "Sorry, we didn't want to upset your girlfriend, we don't mean to hit you, you have enough with that girlfriend!" It turned out that they wanted to apologize for the way they behaved. I know the story doesn't seem logical, but that doesn't matter to a woman. You have to be sure it was real when you tell your stories and convey your emotions. (In the example above, it has more of an impact to use a complaining voice when imitating teenage boys, for example.)

*Don't use my stories, use yours!*

If you are in the waiting room of a dental clinic (as it was a few months ago), ask her if she has seen that particular dentist before and what is her opinion of him (as I did with this girl, I got her number and we were ... for ... the next day, have a great time, first to have a coffee - then to go shopping - then to a bar.

Then-my-house-followed-sex-and after-several hours on my couch watching movies of romance). Tell yourself that you should be cautious these days about dentists because of this, a dentist named Dr. Finger who had the fattest toes you have ever seen in your life. (At this point, she should laugh.)

You can talk about how you think it is interesting that people make their occupations adjustable with their last names. Dr. Finger was a dentist. You also knew a girl named Amy Salmon who went into fish conservation. At this point, if the girl is worth talking about, she will share strange, similar coincidences or talk about something else to keep the conversation going. This is a way to gauge their availability to you if the conversation becomes two-way.

(The woman who does not make the conversation with you is not interested in you, she will not even give a choice, or she is just nervous. If it is the last one, please just take the girl's phone number and see another opportunity. It is difficult to have sex on the same day with a nervous chick.) Once you've made your opening comment and she answers, let the conversation flow. Change the subject. Talk about anything else that is on your mind, such as something that interests you; just read today's psychology. The key is to talk about more than one topic.

Why do you want to do this? Because you want her (and you) to have the feeling that the two of you can talk about anything. You have always been in a conversation like the one that seems to last for hours because you and the other person keep thinking about the new links about the conversation. That is the kind of rapport you want to create.

You can perpetually go backward to the previous conversational links, open them again, and talk about them further. This is to give you a perfect opportunity to avoid awkward pauses. No matter how alpha male you decide to talk about yourself, your attitude will be the most important thing. If you feel fear, she will detect that and will be rejected by you.

Approach, with the full wisdom that women love sex, and thus there is a good chance that a woman will appreciate you when you talk to her. Even if she doesn't, it is her responsibility to let you know, not your attempts to read her mind. If you have a normal conversation, be relaxed and let it flow.

The dirty little secret about your interactions with women is that it doesn't matter what you say. You want to vibrate with her and get the report. Go for the good report.

When it comes time for her to ask your name, say your name with pride and give her a chance to say hers. If you feel like her, shake your hand at this point. This presents the dynamic that it is comfortable to touch. Ask questions; do stories, and just vibrate for a few minutes. You will know that she is interested in the conversation as soon as she begins to do stories on herself answering your previous questions (in other words, as I say, the conversation will become two-way.)

At this point, you have a kind of normal conversation that you would have with friends you have known for a long time. (Although you have not known this woman for more than several minutes, you want her to feel comfortable as if she knew about you.) When you've known someone for a long time, don't bombard them with questions. Instead, you make stories (talk) about what's going on around you, just like you can't believe how much junk food people buy at the store in the afternoon.

Lean back and vibrate with her. I find that I am more prosperous when I am with lower energy than high energy. The reasons are:

- She won't feel as if she has to match your emotional state if you come in very energetic.
- Women are more sexual when they are relaxed.

# MAKING THE APPOINTMENT

When the conversation flows from both parties, and you feel a good vibe, it is time to seal the deal. You can go right then or get a phone number and have your date later.

Base the decision on whether the two of you have time for this point (the date). As a common rule of thumb, it's best to avoid going on a date unless you have enough time. So if she has an appointment in mind, get her phone number and set a date later.

Setting the date (the good one) makes it informal and makes it sound like it's going to be fast and not a business (boring, I think). Say something like, "You know, I'm in the mood for a cup of coffee. I'd love for you to join me."

Rules are important; here is a summary:

1.     Give it a sense that they won't be around long. This will positively affect any doubts you may have about having coffee (or what) with a guy you will meet.

2.     Make it sound casual. You don't want her to think of a date in the traditional sense, or else she will get in the traditional nervous dynamics and make you wait for sex (most have a policy of not having sex with a man on the first date.)

If you decide to get her phone number, just say something like, "I enjoyed talking to you, but I have to go now. Maybe we can go out sometime. " If she says something positive like "sounds nice," then ask for a cell phone number.

As an alpha male, you control the frame and do not negotiate if she doesn't want it. It is always better to approach a woman alone, from a woman with typical friends who will not leave her to separate with a guy who barely knows her to separate with an individual as soon as they satisfy her. (If she wants to go, the group will interfere.)

If the woman you board is with a group, I find the best way to handle it is to get her phone number and meet her later.

# TELEPHONE SUCCESS

In typical relationship books, you'll find all kinds of no-call rules for three days. Since you are an alpha male, you move through life and do not want to play games, So, call whenever you want.

Indeed, I have found from experience that it is better to call EARLIER than LATER. Call her that night or the next day if you want. That way, your conversation with her is still fresh on her mind. When you call, you need to play positively and comfortably with who you are. Remember, you are not forcing on her, but instead, you give the honor and the privilege of talking to you.

Each person is different, there are usually some rules that you should know when you call, but there are some rules. One method I have found to relax and not overthink the conversation is to do some activity while on the phone. Maybe eat a bag of potatoes ... Or call her while you're driving or walking your dog. When you are sitting at home not doing something, you can have seconds of doubts.

When you call, a roommate or family might answer the phone. Most guys say when they call, in a nervous tone of voice, "Hi, is [the girl] there?" When you do that, a lot of people's automatic response is to go defensive and cockblocky and say something nice (if they're nice), "Who's calling, please?"

This makes you take a step back, and when you talk to your girl, you will come across as nervous and therefore unattractive. A better way to deal with your roommate or family is to be relaxed when you call and when someone answers, for example, "Hi, this is [your name]. I'm looking for [your girl's name] to call."

If your girl is the one who answers the phone, that's perfect. Jump down to where you're going. If someone else (who is not your girl), talk to them amicably. Keep the conversation light and lighthearted. It will make your life sort of magnitude easier if you are with friends who live with it. If they tell you the girl is not here, they offer to take a message, say, "Thanks, but I'm leaving a message." Trust me, and they'll say they called her. Not leaving a message adds an air of mystery.

Most dating books are wrong when they say the rush to get to the phone. Unless you're in a rush, don't feel like you have to follow such rules. Continue your comfortable frame as an alpha male. You're calling because you want to chat in confidence, not because you're desperate for a date and have to think to pretend you're busy.

Also, you will find a lot of advice online on how to talk to girls on cell phone numbers, but my advice is to ignore some. Individuals will have to tell stories from their own lives, and you will adopt them as your own. However, this is a huge error because you come across as false. It must be original; Talk about your own life with the girls you call.

When your girl is on the phone, don't force the conversation; instead, just keep chatting about the conversation you had with her when you got her number. Get back to those conversational threads for a little bit. When you do this, you will return her to the state she was in when she met you. Then start telling interesting stories about something that happened to you in your life. Your goal is to be light and witty and just "vibrate" with the girl.

Make sure you speak with animated sounds and not filtered. Don't use monotonous things or low volume when speaking. Avoid talking about things that make you nervous when you talk. That includes things such as asking her "WHAT'S SHE UP TO," asking how her day was (instead of telling her how YOUR day was), and tell her that you are the guy who knows her from the bookstore (or wherever you met her)...

Don't try hard to create a report. Better, just assume that the report already exists. This is the way you can relax and have an interesting conversation. After they chatted for a while, meeting the girl will be easy. She will probably always do it indirectly. Just say something like, "Hey, I'm busy with work, but it would be fun to go out for coffee for a minute. When are you free?"

(Obviously, your goal is not to go out with her for just a little bit, but don't say this to her. You tell her that your time is limited to lower her defenses against having sex on the first date. )

If she gets defensive or gives you a negative answer, don't worry about it. At least you had 10 or 15 minutes practicing how to talk on the phone with a girl; now you hardly know.

Just say, "It was a pleasure talking to you. I guess I'll talk to you later." Don't end up saying, "Hey, I'll call you this week." The former puts you more of a challenge and unpredictable in their eyes. When you are talking to a woman "hand in hand," it is time to escalate the interaction towards sex slightly. Realize that women want sex almost as much as we do, and you just do it. There are five things you are going to focus on:

1)   Stay relaxed as much as possible (that is, the opposite of nervous and insecure).
2)   Feel sexual and hot.
3)   Talk like their old friends.
4)   Taking the initiative and persisting towards romance.

# CONVERSATION SUCCESSFUL ON A DATE

You want your conversation to be free, fluid, and not forced, so keep your speech informal, just as if you were talking with a friend. Keep in mind that you are patiently getting to know her a little before taking action. Relax, and don't think too much about what to say.

*Here are some amazing recommendations on what to talk about:*

Interesting stories from your life.
She will probably start talking about something interesting in her life. If something she says is fascinating to you, tell her you'd like to hear more about it. However, do not pretend to be interested in something, as women can often detect falsehood.

Relevant facts from your past.
Make these relevant events something emotionally huge, just as it was something very interesting that you saw, or something scandalous or out of the place where it happened. She will probably tell her relevant facts.

TV shows, movies, and celebrities.

Even if you don't spend much time watching TV, you can catch up quickly by watching a few minutes on the news channels or the Internet. The Hollywood A-List website at www.thehollywoodalist.com is a celebrity gossip source that can give you an easy conversation with almost most women.

Music.
Look at Rolling Stone magazine to quickly find out about today's music and how you can interestingly talk about music.

Food.
It doesn't matter if a woman is fat or thin; the chances are high that she is obsessed with this topic.

Holidays.
Talk about the most interesting aspects of the places you have been to.

Your passions in life.
Do you have passions? Or not? If you don't have them, develop some. And develop the ability to talk about them.

# SIGNS OF ATTRACTION

I probably don't need to list the attraction signals that you find in relationship books. The reason is if a woman is clinging around you, talking to you, and being nice, obviously she doesn't dislike you!

Prior it's always possible that she likes you just as a friend (even though the more you keep pushing, the interaction backs off), so my advice is to learn and memorize the following list I have released and then try to forget it. And this is because you will paralyze yourself during conversations if you start by analyzing small details like how forcefully she twirls her hair around her fingers.

Once you have enough experience with women, you will instinctively recognize the signs of attraction. The following list is in no particular order.

1. She compliments you on just about anything.
2. She is nervous around you. Look for signs of nervousness, such ashis muscles stretching.
3. She taunts you playfully.
4. She attempts to tell you how much she admires the same things thatyou like
5. She talks about things you can do in the future. "Do you also likevintage clothing stores? she might say, "We should go someday!" By the way,

this is additionally something you should share with the girls. Could you not do it too seriously? Do it like you are playful. "We could go shopping for the tightest purple pimp-looking clothes on Fifth Avenue."
6. When her legs are crossed, see at the foot of her top leg. If he ispointing at you, it is a sign that you have obtained his full attention.
7. She makes an effort to keep the conversation moving forward whenit quiets down. (Now and then, you can even test her attraction on purpose by allowing the conversation to pause or end on your part.

Then see if she restarts the conversation)
8. She touches her face. When a person touches their face, it is a signthat they are thinking about something. To be sure that she is thinking good thoughts, look for this signal combined with others on the list.
9. She fixes her gaze on your eyes and keeps her gaze
10.She imitates you. (Being passive by nature, women follow the lead of a man they are attracted to.) Watch to see how she does.

- The posture is similar to yours.

- Modulate the volume of his voice to match yours.
- Modulate the scale of his voice to match yours.
- Match the rhythm of your breathing.- Laugh when you laugh.

11.Peel a cylindrical object such as a wine glass or pencil from top to bottom with your thumb and index finger. This means that you are having a strong effect on her, big boy!

12.She moves her head back or sides. Watch her hair sway as she does that.

13.She touches his face while he looks at you.

14.She hangs her shoe off her foot or even takes it off.

15. She rubs her fingertips around the top of her chest

16. She rubs her palm on the rear of her head, letting her hair fluff.

17. She plays with her hair while she sees you.

18.She shows a genuine smile rather than a forced one.

19. Her eyes glow because her pupils are large and dilated 20. She raises her eyebrows at times.

21. Her nipples harden. Of course, you can only say this if she is wearing the right clothes.

22. She has a relaxed face. (However, sometimes a non-relaxed facecan be fine, like when a woman is so attracted to you that she feels nervous)

23. She fixes her gaze on your eyes. Your pupils dilate (grow)

24. She focuses her attention on you, even when other people are around.

25. She touches you while speaking to you. Even if it is "accidental,"Ladies are highly mindful of their bodies, so this will rarely be an accident when they touch you. Watch her touch your arm to emphasize a point or stroke her feet against yours when she laughs at one of your witty comments.

26. She laughs at your comments like they're the funniest things they'veever heard, even if they are only mildly resourceful.

27. She shows her tongue, such as when she touches it with her frontteeth or wets her lips

28. With her body bent towards you, she quickly sits upright, her armmuscles tense and her chest lifted.

29. She shows her palms towards you. Open palms indicate that shefeels open to you

30. She rubs her wrist or plays with her bracelet.

31. Your skin becomes flushed. Watch particularly to notice if she blushes. (This can also be a sign that she's feeling horny.)

32. She rubs her earlobes or works with her earrings.

33. She asks about herself. They will not be just superficial questionsthat she has asked anyone ("Where are you from?"), On the contrary, they will be deeper questions to determine what makes you tick (example: What are your passions in life?) 34. She is energetic when she talks to you.

35. Your voice becomes a little lower (half an octave or about)

36. She adjusts her blouse.

There are some signals that a woman gives to indicate that she is not interested in you. Usually, these signals are subconscious; women do not always think about them. Sometimes women do it in an exaggerated way to try to give you a hint.

Beware in your mind as you need to see several of these signals manifesting before drawing any conclusions. A person sometimes crosses their arms simply because they are cold rather than uncomfortable.

As well, try to get a woman to express her rejection of you in words. On multiple occasions, I have had a woman send me signals of rejection. However, I persisted in the conversation and eventually managed to fuck her.

1.	A soft hand (shaking hands without strength, without interest).
2.	She looks elsewhere, especially when you're talking to her.
3.	She makes little effort to talk to you. Give one-word answers.
4.	Crossing arms across your chest (putting them as a barrier.

5.	Cross your legs at the ankles.
6.	She is continually scratching his nose. When a person is uncomfortable, blood collects in their nose, making them itch.
7.	When you turn your body language towards her, she leans back and away from you.
8.	She seems off talking to you.
9.	She has a neutral tone of voice.

Assume right now that you always attract a woman to you. Not even interpersonal relationships are exact and fulfilled prophecies; they are based on our attitudes, so use that to your advantage. If you have a strong inner attitude that says, "Of course she is attracted to me," then she will catch your wave and be influenced by you.

# HOW TO MAKE A WOMAN FEEL HAPPY AND VERY HOT FOR SEX

what you would like sex to appear in her as if it happened spontaneously. After all, she was only coming to your place for a few minutes, right? If you go to your place or his, save the conversation of the subject you were talking about. When you get out of the car in the parking lot or on the driveway, save the topic.

When you walk to the door, save the conversation. It's his way of keeping her emotionally focused. Do not pause the conversation, or else she will begin to think, and when she thinks about the situation, by logic, it may be that emotion overcomes her; in this case, you will hear the dreaded words, "I need you to give me a clue."
And at this point, you need to give her a comfortable idea that you are alone and in isolation. If you're at home, make him overly fascinated with his library of books and DVD collection. If you are in your home, show him all the cool and interesting stuff you have.

You have cool and interesting stuff in your home, right? If not, get some stuff! Anything that you can have a conversation that you can talk about would be nice to have at the show:

- The table of reserved cafes on the places where you have been traveling.
- Albures made by your great aunt.
- Interesting Reports (of those that have interesting topics to talk about, suchas Psychology Today and Hospitality Weekly, not like Maxim and Playboy) • Floors. Two plants that are tough-killer and that look good are the jade tree and the cast iron plant.

Keep your home safe. It was not necessarily as if it was something made for the eye of a strict guy, but at least having it as if it would not fail a health department inspection. Haver pictures on the wall rather than a poster. Have clean sheets on your bed. Have decent furniture. Clean and sweep your floors with the vacuum cleaner. Wash the dishes. How to demonstrate that, in your home, you can have conversations in each room.

# EASY ALPHA MALE EXERCISE

Take a walk around your house and think about the conversational topics that you can have from each place; For example, "you wouldn't believe how I ended up being the owner of the one with the sculpture on the corner."

A friend of mine gave me some good advice about the bedroom, that is, you should avoid calling it a "bedroom." Why? Because the word "bedroom" is a weapon of great proportion programmed in your mind by our purification society to say, "Uh oh, Sex alarm!"

And its place extends its definition. My friend calls his bedroom "the meditation room. I was calling it that, I have observed that as well (you can even make her smile by calling it that, you can get a giggle out of her), and you can talk about how you like to go to your mediation site and to remain silent sometimes thinking-contemplating.

Find an excuse for you to sit very close to each other in your living room or bedroom.
I haven't glad to tell you, "Take a look at my photo album; I have an awesome photograph from my last blah-blah vacation...," which is why you'll be sitting hip-to-hip on

your couch as you walk around and peek through the most interesting photos.

These movies are fantastic. They give you an appointment and a half of time on the couch next to her as you progress towards sex. Put on a movie if you can. It could be any kind of movie that will be pretty, but find light comedies such as Ghostbusters if possible.

# BY THE WAY, GHOSTBUSTERS IS A GREAT MOVIE TO WATCH WITH THE GIRL YOU JUST BROUGHT INTO YOUR HOME BECAUSE:

1)It is a movie of which everyone has fond memories, during all these years.

2)There are many points about sexual arousal in this movie.

One of the best sex preludes you can encounter with a woman is the standard "getting ready" in the couch position. The other is sitting together to touch hip to hip with your arm behind her with your back resting on the cushions.

Suppose you let a while pass. Sexually, the woman is like iron. She will slowly warm up. Man, however, can be turned on and off in the same way that a light switch is turned on and off. Then, what do you need to do to heat it slowly? You must gradually progress from one level to the next. Be sure not to make very fast moves or plays that she cannot warm up; this way, sex won't happen.

At a certain point when you're with her, touch her lightly on her shoulder with your hand and stretch her back. A bit slower, put your hand on her collar in a more secure way; if she is interested in you, she will hug you or snuggle with you.

If she doesn't do that to herself, don't allow yourself to feel down or upset. Instead, relax and feel good. Now stretch your arm and put it behind her almost, listen to me well, almost touching her (that your arm continued to touch the sofa), and try the former again after a while. Eventually, her feverish state will reach a point where she is dying from putting your arm around her.

Quiet hands. Put your arm around her. Move her silky hair, enjoying the feel of the hair sliding between your fingers. Breathe and smell her hair sensually. There are things you can do when you are with her to go far. Keep in mind the following parts of her body ... even if they are erogenous zones.

1.   THEIR HAIR. THE BEST WAY TO WARM UP A WOMAN IS BYTOUCHING OR STROKING HER HAIR.

2.   Touch your scalp. It's good, and only this is very erogenous.

3.   The inside of her elbows. The touch with your fingertips can makeher shake.

4.   The skin between her fingers. When you hold a woman's hand, thebest way to do it is by locking your fingers with hers; it would be to interlock their fingers with yours.

5.   Her ears. When you are about to kiss her, and you are very close toher, blow gently into her ears, touch the edges of her ear with the tip of your finger.

6.   her shoulders.

7.   Her feet.

8.   Her toes.

*Knock all the mentioned*
*areas on her body, and*
*she will start to wake up*
*the way we want.*

And so things start to get hotter and hotter, move your face to his hair and inhale deeply And say: "Mmmmm, I love the way your hair smells ..." the interaction gets hotter and hotter, and you have your arms around her; the two of you will be looking very deeply into each other's eyes, perhaps with each other's mouths slightly ajar. At this point, you should always lightly brush your bottom lip gently against his, and you will see all his melt in a kiss with you.

continue your kissing process; don't just stick your tongue in his mouth. Expect her to give you a bit of her tongue and then exchange, slowly and then soon, the two of you will be giving each other a passionate kiss.

Have you ever felt very nervous about kissing a girl for the first time and in the direct way that I described it? You, too, can indirectly go to that situation by mentioning this, using what I call the technique: "Rate My Kiss. Yes, that is how the "Tarifa Mi Beso" technique works. When you feel that the moment that has been generated is conducive to the kiss, you have to say, "How much would you score on the scale of 1 to 10 in your ability to kiss?" She can answer you, or she can not answer you, but in 95% of the cases, women will open their lips, and you will be able to move your face towards her.

# CLOSING WORDS: BECOMING AN ALPHA MALE

It's almost impossible to be an alpha male as long as you follow someone else's orders. When you have someone telling you what to do and do it, you are the beta of that situation. There are only two ways to handle it, and both have their merits.

First, you can play the game. Do your job, take your boss's orders, get paid, and hopefully, you will climb the corporate ladder. The downsides are that you will have to follow office policy to get anywhere, and your boss may fire you if you don't kiss his ass.

Situations like this are not the best in the world for a man's sense of selfworth. And by the way, aggressively flirting with that beautiful secretary can get you off the hook. Top management guys don't like it when lower-level guys go after "their" women. So live your romantic life outside of the workplace. (In fact, the best strategy at work is always to have women working for you. That frees you from trouble.) The second way is to ditch everything and start your own business. This involves a ton more risk, but at least you'll be in charge of your destiny.

That is the path that I chose at age 29, leaving the corporate environment to become an inventor, and I never regretted it. I had some difficult years financially, but I did well, getting the business going. Money aside, the bottom line is that I don't take orders from anyone.

# BE THE BOSS!

To add some leadership positions in your life. It doesn't matter if you're just a graduate aide in a college class. Being in a position of authority somewhere turns women on. Have running your own business and to be the boss of employees are great places to be there. When there are people who are following you, you acquire alpha status.

By the way, a great place to have a meeting with a woman is somewhere where you are the boss. One strategy for this is to say to the woman, "Stop by my office, and we'll go for a coffee there."

When she shows up, she will see that you are an important man who people follow and who is in command, giving her alpha status.